First World War
and Army of Occupation
War Diary
France, Belgium and Germany

36 DIVISION
109 Infantry Brigade
Royal Inniskilling Fusiliers
10th Battalion
4 October 1915 - 31 January 1918

WO95/2510/4

The Naval & Military Press Ltd
www.nmarchive.com
Published in association with The National Archives

Published by

The Naval & Military Press Ltd

Unit 10 Ridgewood Industrial Park,

Uckfield, East Sussex,

TN22 5QE England

Tel: +44 (0) 1825 749494

www.naval-military-press.com

www.nmarchive.com

This diary has been reprinted in facsimile from the original. Any imperfections are inevitably reproduced and the quality may fall short of modern type and cartographic standards.

© **Crown Copyright**
Images reproduced by permission of The National Archives, London, England, 2015.

Contents

Document type	Place/Title	Date From	Date To
Heading	WO95/2510/4		
Heading	36th Division 109th Infy. Bde 10th Bn. Roy. Innis. Fus. Oct 1915-Jan 1918		
Heading	36th Div 10th R. Innis. Fus. First Portion. Of Vol I To Nov 28th		
War Diary	Boulogne	04/10/1915	07/10/1915
War Diary	Coisy	07/10/1915	17/10/1915
War Diary	Beauval	20/10/1915	21/10/1915
War Diary	Collin	26/10/1915	26/10/1915
War Diary	Hebuterne	27/10/1915	01/11/1915
War Diary	Colin	02/11/1915	02/11/1915
War Diary	Beauval	03/11/1915	26/11/1915
War Diary	Gorenflos	27/11/1915	28/11/1915
Heading	36 Div. 10th R. Inniskg. Fus. Vol 23 To Dec 31		
War Diary	Gorenflos	29/11/1915	31/12/1915
Miscellaneous	36 10th R. Inniskg. Fus. Vol 4		
War Diary	Gorenflos	01/01/1916	05/01/1916
War Diary	Bonneville	06/01/1916	03/02/1916
War Diary	Toutencourt	05/02/1916	05/02/1916
War Diary	Acheux	06/02/1916	24/02/1916
War Diary	Trenches	24/02/1916	26/02/1916
War Diary	Acheux	28/02/1916	29/02/1916
War Diary	Forceville	29/02/1916	29/02/1916
Heading	War Diary of 10th (S) Rst. Royal Innis. Fus. from 1st to 31st March 1916 (Volume 6)		
War Diary	Acheux	02/03/1916	03/03/1916
War Diary	Martinsart	03/03/1916	09/03/1916
War Diary	Trenches	10/03/1916	13/03/1916
War Diary	Martinsart	13/03/1916	16/03/1916
War Diary	Trenches	19/03/1916	25/03/1916
War Diary	Martinsart	25/03/1916	31/03/1916
Heading	War Diary 10th (S) Bn. R. Innis Fusrs. From 1st April 1916 To 30th April 1916		
War Diary	Thiepval Wood	01/04/1916	06/04/1916
War Diary	Martinsart	08/04/1916	12/04/1916
War Diary	Thiepval Wood	15/04/1916	18/04/1916
War Diary	Martinsart	19/04/1916	30/04/1916
Operation(al) Order(s)	Battalion Order No. 10 By Lieut-Col. W.F. Hessey, Commanding 11th (S) Bn. Rl. Inniskilling Fus. 2nd April 1916	02/04/1916	02/04/1916
Operation(al) Order(s)	Battalion Order No. 11 By Lieut-Col. W.F. Hessey, Commanding 11th (S) Bn. Rl. Inniskilling Fus. 2nd April 1916	08/04/1916	08/04/1916
Operation(al) Order(s)	Battalion Order No. 12 By Lieut-Col. W.F. Hessey, Commanding 11th (S) Bn. Rl. Inniskilling Fus. 14.4.16	14/04/1916	14/04/1916
Miscellaneous	Relief Orders By Lt. Col. Ross Smyth, Comdg. 10th Bn. Royal Innis Fus.	29/04/1916	29/04/1916
Operation(al) Order(s)	Battalion Orders No. 16 By Major The Earl Of Leitrim Commanding 11th (S) Bn. Rl. Inniskilling Fus. 29.4.16	29/04/1916	29/04/1916

Heading	War Diary Of 10th (S) Battn. Royal Inniskilling Fus. From 1/5/16 To 31/5/16		
War Diary	Martinsart	01/05/1916	08/05/1916
War Diary	Lealvillers	08/05/1916	31/05/1916
Heading	109th Brigade 36th Division 1/10th Battalion Royal Inniskilling Fusiliers June 1916		
War Diary	Lealvillers	01/06/1916	19/06/1916
War Diary		14/06/1916	16/06/1916
War Diary	Forceville	20/06/1916	30/06/1916
War Diary	Forceville	27/06/1916	27/06/1916
Heading	109th Brigade 36th Division 1/10th Battalion Royal Inniskilling Fusiliers July 1916		
Miscellaneous			
War Diary		02/07/1916	27/07/1916
Map	War Diary Of 11th (3) Bn. RE. Inniskilling Fusiliers July 1916		
Heading	War Diary Of 10th (S) Battalion Royal Inniskilling Fusiliers For Month Of August 1916 Vol 11		
War Diary	Ploegsteert Wood	02/08/1916	31/08/1916
Miscellaneous	Battalion Orders By Major F.S.N. Macrory, Commanding 10th (S) Battalion Royal Inniskilling Fus.	03/08/1916	03/08/1916
Miscellaneous	Acquittance Roll (All Arms)		
Miscellaneous			
Miscellaneous	Acquittance Roll (All Arms)		
Miscellaneous	Battalion Orders By Major F.S.N. Macrory, Commanding 10th Battalion Royal Inniskilling Fusiliers	14/08/1916	14/08/1916
Miscellaneous	Relief Orders By Lieut-Colonel F.S.N. Macrory, Commanding 10th (S) Battn. Royal Inniskilling Fus.		
Miscellaneous	Relief Orders By Lieut-Colonel F.S.N. Macrory Commanding 10th (S) Battalion Royal Inniskilling Fusiliers	27/08/1916	27/08/1916
Heading	War Diary Of 10th Bn. Royal Inniskilling Fusiliers From 1st September 1916 To 30th September 1916		
War Diary	Ploegsteert	01/09/1916	30/09/1916
Miscellaneous	Battalion Order By Lieut-Colonel F.S.N. Macrory, Commanding 10th Battalion Royal Inniskilling Fuslrs.	03/09/1916	03/09/1916
Miscellaneous	Relief Orders By Lieut-Colonel F.S.N. Macrory, Commanding 10th Battalion Royal Inniskilling Fusiliers	11/09/1916	11/09/1916
Miscellaneous	Relief Orders By Lieut-Colonel F.S.N. Macrory, Commanding 10th Battalion Royal Inniskilling Fus.	17/09/1916	17/09/1916
Heading	War Diary Of 10th Battalion Royal Inniskilling Fusiliers For Period From 1st October 1916 To 31st October 1916 Vol 11		
War Diary		01/10/1916	31/10/1916
Miscellaneous	Relief Orders By Major R.S. Knox. Commanding 10th Bn. Royal Inniskilling Fusiliers	05/10/1916	05/10/1916
Miscellaneous	Relief Orders By Major R.S. Knox Commanding 10th Bn. Royal Inniskilling Fuslrs	11/10/1916	11/10/1916
Miscellaneous	Relief Orders By Lieut-Colonel F.S.N. Macrory Commanding 10th Battalion Royal Inniskilling Fusiliers	20/10/1916	20/10/1916
Miscellaneous	Relief Orders By Lt. Colonel F.S.N. Macrory, Commdg. 10th (Service) Battn. Royal Inniskilling Fusiliers	23/10/1916	23/10/1916
Miscellaneous			
Heading	War Diary Of 10th Royal Inniskilling Fusiliers From 1st November 1916 To 30th November 1916 Vol 12		

Type	Description	Start	End
War Diary		01/11/1916	30/11/1916
War Diary		08/11/1916	21/11/1916
Miscellaneous	Relief Orders By Lieut-Colonel F.S.N. Macrory, Commanding 10th Battalion Royal Inniskilling Fuslrs	04/11/1916	04/11/1916
Miscellaneous	Relief Orders By Lieut-Colonel F.S.N. Macrory, Commanding 10th Battalion Royal Inniskilling Fusiliers	11/11/1916	11/11/1916
Miscellaneous	Reference 109th. Brigade Order No. 1	16/11/1916	16/11/1916
Miscellaneous	Relief Orders By Lieut-Colonel F.S.N. Macrory Commanding 10th Bn. Royal Inniskilling Fusiliers	25/11/1916	25/11/1916
Miscellaneous	Relief Orders By Lieut. Colonel F.S.N. Macrory, Commdg. 10th Battn. Royal Inniskilling Fusiliers	28/11/1916	28/11/1916
Heading	War Diary Of 10th Battalion Royal Inniskilling Fusiliers From 1st December 1916 To 31st December 1916 Vol 13		
War Diary		05/12/1916	21/12/1916
War Diary	Ploegsteert Wood U19.6 20.85 (Map Ref. 28 S.W.4 Ed. 3d 1/10,000	10/12/1916	31/12/1916
War Diary	Ploegsteert Wood U19.6 20.85 (Map Ref. 28 S.W.4 Ed. 3d 1/10,000	28/12/1916	28/12/1916
Miscellaneous	Relief Orders By Major R.S. Knox Commanding 10th R. Innis. Fusrs	28/12/1916	28/12/1916
Miscellaneous	Trench Store List. Taken Over By From		
Heading	War Diary Of 10th Royal Inniskilling Fusiliers From 1st January 1917 To 31st January 1917 Vol 14		
War Diary	Ploegsteert Wood Hyde Park Corner U.19.G.30.80	01/01/1917	22/01/1917
War Diary	Ploegsteert Wood	24/01/1917	31/01/1917
Heading	War Diary Of 10th Battalion Royal Innis, Fusiliers From 1st February 1917 To 28th February 1917 Vol 15		
War Diary	Ploegsteert Wood U.19.a.2.G. U.8. And U.14	01/02/1917	26/02/1917
War Diary	Bulford Camp T.20.c.4.1	27/02/1917	28/02/1917
Heading	War Diary Of 10th Battalion Royal Innis. Fusiliers From 1st March 1917 To 31st March 1917 Vol 16		
War Diary	Bulford Camp	01/03/1917	18/03/1917
War Diary	Meteren	19/03/1917	20/03/1917
War Diary	Morbecque	21/03/1917	21/03/1917
War Diary	Hallines	22/03/1917	22/03/1917
War Diary	Acquin	23/03/1917	31/03/1917
Heading	War Diary Of 10th Battalion Royal Inniskilling Fusiliers From 1st April 1917 Till 30th April 1917 Vol 17		
War Diary	Acquin	01/04/1917	04/04/1917
War Diary	Hallines	05/04/1917	05/04/1917
War Diary	Hazebrouck	06/04/1917	06/04/1917
War Diary	Wakefield Huts Near Locre	07/04/1917	07/04/1917
War Diary	Spanbroek Sector	08/04/1917	18/04/1917
War Diary	Hazebrouck Sector	19/04/1917	20/04/1917
War Diary	Kemmel	21/04/1917	26/04/1917
War Diary	Spanbroek Sector	27/04/1917	30/04/1917
Heading	War Diary Of 10th Battalion Royal Inniskilling Fusiliers From 1st May, 1917 Till 31st May. 1917 Vol 18		
War Diary	Spanbroek Sector (Brigade Right Sector)	01/05/1917	02/05/1917
War Diary	Spanbroek Sector	02/05/1917	02/05/1917
War Diary	Kemmel	03/05/1917	07/05/1917
War Diary	Spanbroek Sector	07/05/1917	13/05/1917
War Diary	Wakefield Huts	14/05/1917	31/05/1917
Heading	War Diary For Month Of June 1917 10th Royal Inniskilling Fusiliers Vol 19		

War Diary	Wakefield Huts	01/06/1917	01/06/1917
War Diary	Berthen Area	02/06/1917	06/06/1917
War Diary	Spanbroek Sector	07/06/1917	08/06/1917
War Diary	Wakefield Huts	09/06/1917	12/06/1917
War Diary	Mont Noir	13/06/1917	17/06/1917
War Diary	Weston Camp Near Locre	18/06/1917	18/06/1917
War Diary	Spanbroek Sector	19/06/1917	29/06/1917
War Diary	De Zon Camp Near Locre	29/06/1917	30/06/1917
Heading	10th Royal Inniskilling Fusiliers War Diary For Month Of July. 1917 Vol 20		
War Diary	De Zon Camp Near Locre	01/07/1917	01/07/1917
War Diary	Caestre	02/07/1917	05/07/1917
War Diary	Hondeghem Area	06/07/1917	06/07/1917
War Diary	Arques	07/07/1917	07/07/1917
War Diary	Haut Loquin	08/07/1917	26/07/1917
War Diary	Winnezeele Area	27/07/1917	30/07/1917
War Diary	Hiphoek	31/07/1917	31/07/1917
War Diary		01/07/1917	01/07/1917
Miscellaneous	10th Battalion Royal Inniskilling Fusiliers	14/07/1917	14/07/1917
Miscellaneous	Narrative		
War Diary	War Diary 10th Royal Inniskilling Fusiliers For Month Of August 1917 Vol 21		
War Diary	Hiphoek	01/08/1917	04/08/1917
War Diary	Vlamertinghe	05/08/1917	07/08/1917
War Diary	Ypres	08/08/1917	12/08/1917
War Diary	Vlamertinghe	13/08/1917	17/08/1917
War Diary	Winnezeele	18/08/1917	24/08/1917
War Diary	Haplincourt	25/08/1917	28/08/1917
War Diary	Ytres Area	29/08/1917	29/08/1917
War Diary	Bertincourt	30/08/1917	31/08/1917
War Diary		01/08/1917	01/08/1917
Map	G.3		
Miscellaneous	Message Form		
Miscellaneous	U.X.I. Brigade		
Miscellaneous	Platoon Company Battalion		
Heading	War Diary Of 10th Battalion Royal Inniskilling Fusiliers Period 1st September 1917 To 30th September 1917 Vol 22		
War Diary	Bertincourt P.D.b.	01/09/1917	02/09/1917
War Diary	Bertincourt	03/09/1917	06/09/1917
War Diary	Hermies	07/09/1917	14/09/1917
War Diary	Bertincourt	15/09/1917	22/09/1917
War Diary	Hermies	23/09/1917	30/09/1917
War Diary	Bertincourt	01/10/1917	08/10/1917
War Diary	Hermies	09/10/1917	16/10/1917
War Diary	Bertincourt	17/10/1917	24/10/1917
War Diary	Hermies	25/10/1917	31/10/1917
War Diary	Achiet-Le-Petit	01/12/1917	01/12/1917
War Diary	Bertincourt	02/12/1917	11/12/1917
War Diary	Metz	12/11/1917	13/11/1917
War Diary	Sorel	14/11/1917	15/11/1917
War Diary		16/12/1917	16/12/1917
War Diary	Halloy	17/12/1917	29/12/1917
War Diary	Demuin	30/12/1917	31/12/1917
Heading	10th Royal Inniskilling Fusiliers War Diary For Month Of January 1918 Vol 26		

Heading	War Diary Of 10th (Service) Battalion Royal Inniskilling Fusiliers		
War Diary	Demuin	01/01/1918	07/01/1918
War Diary	Beaucourt	08/01/1918	09/01/1918
War Diary	Nesle	10/01/1918	11/01/1918
War Diary	Gd Seraucourt	12/01/1918	13/01/1918
War Diary	Battalion In The Line	14/01/1918	18/01/1918
War Diary	Battalion In Support	18/01/1918	21/01/1918
War Diary	Battalion In The Line	22/01/1918	27/01/1918
War Diary	Bn. In Reserve	28/01/1918	28/01/1918
War Diary	Fluquieres	29/01/1918	31/01/1918

WD 95/2510 (4)

WD 95/2510 (4)

36TH DIVISION
109TH INFY. BDE

10TH BN ROY. INNIS. FUS.

OCT 1915-JAN 1918

DISBANDED

Box 2510

36th K'n

10/36

To R. Hmh R. ? Pao:
First portion of Vol I
t Nov 28

4948/12/1

1. P.
10 sheets

Army Form C. 2118.

Further
[?]

WAR DIARY
or
INTELLIGENCE SUMMARY.
(Erase heading not required.)

10th 13th Royal Inniskilling

Place	Date 1915	Hour	Summary of Events and Information	Remarks and references to Appendices
BOULOGNE	Oct 4		(A) Transport, machine Gun Section & Adv. Party under 2nd in Com'd Major G.H. Smith sailed from South SOUTHAMPTON and disembarked at HAVRE.	
	" 5		(B) The Battalion, less above details, under Lt Col. Ross Smyth comdg. sailed from FOLKESTONE and disembarked at 1.30 am on 6th Oct/15 at BOULOGNE, where it went under canvas at a Rest Camp distant 2 miles from the quay.	
			Strength (B) Battalion	
			Transport, M.G. Sect etc (A)	
			Total	
			Officers 4 26 30	
			Other Ranks 109 890 999	
			113 916 1029	
			In addition to the above 16 men of the K.O.Y.L.I. were taken overseas under escort.	
	" 6	8.30am	1 French Interpreter attached for duties.	
		2 pm	Bn Battalion taken for Route March with Band.	

Army Form C. 2118.

WAR DIARY
or
INTELLIGENCE SUMMARY. 10th Bn. Royal Inniskilling Fusiliers

(Erase heading not required.)

Instructions regarding War Diaries and Intelligence Summaries are contained in F.S. Regs., Part II. and the Staff Manual respectively. Title pages will be prepared in manuscript.

Place	Date 1915	Hour	Summary of Events and Information	Remarks and references to Appendices
BOULOGNE	Oct 7	10 am	The Battalion, less 2 sick left in Hospital, entrained at the GARE CENTRAL, BOULOGNE at 10 am	
Coisy	" 7	5.30 pm	Arrived COISY, having detrained at FLESSELLES & proceeded by road, distance approx. 4 miles. Transport, M.G Section & other Details under Major Smith had reached COISY at 2.30 am the same day via AMIENS from HAVRE. The whole Battalion immediately went into billets.	
	" 8		Work commenced on Sanitation & improvement of billets generally. The 16 men of the K.O.Y.L.I. were handed over to an officer of the 14th R. Irish Rifles for escort to their own unit. Head Quarters Details formed into a separate unit for accommodation, Rations & Discipline — The Battalion was thus divided into 6 units, viz 4 Coys, M.G. Sect, & Hd Quarters.	
	" 10		A Brigade Bombing Class was formed.	
	" 12		All entrances & exits of village covered by a system of Coy Guards, for which purpose village divided into areas & passes given to inhabitants vouched for by the acting mayor.	

1577 Wt.W10791/1773 500,000 1/15 D.D. & L. A.D.S.S./Forms/C. 2118.

Army Form C. 2118.

WAR DIARY
or
INTELLIGENCE SUMMARY.
(Erase heading not required.)

10th R. Innuskilling Fusiliers

Place	Date 1915	Hour	Summary of Events and Information	Remarks and references to Appendices
COISY	Oct 13	9.30am	Battalion took part in Brigade Field operations - Attack practice.	
	14		Rifle Range completed. Range of 40 yards, fire from Trench. Musketry commenced.	
			Battalion Bombing classes formed.	practice
	16		Battalion took part in Divisional Field operations - Battle of Encounter.	
	17		Practical demonstration in use of Gas & Gas Helmets given in the chemical advisor to 3rd Army.	
BEAUVAL	20		Battalion moved out of billets COISY at 8.40am with all Transport, less G.S. waggons & a Rear party, to Divisional Rendezvous immediately E of FLESSELLES. On termination of Field operations, involving a movement to the North in artillery formation, the Battalion moved into Billets at BEAUVAL, being joined there by the Rear Party & G.S. waggons.	
	21		Billets found to be an improvement on those at COISY. Work started immediately on Sanitation, incinerators & improvements to billets etc.	
COUIN	26		Battalion, less Guard on Stores & Officers Mess men attending Brigade Bombing Class, marched from BEAUVAL at 8.15am, proceeding via TERRAMESNIL - SARTON - AUTHIE & ST LEGER to COUIN where it went under canvas. Axle of B.Coy's Field Cooker broke just E of ST LEGER. Orders received to move next day to HEBUTERNE for instruction in Trenches.	

Army Form C. 2118.

WAR DIARY
or
INTELLIGENCE SUMMARY.   10th R. Inniskilling Fus.
(Erase heading not required.)

Place	Date	Hour	Summary of Events and Information	Remarks and references to Appendices
HEBUTERNE	1915 Oct 27		at 3.45 pm today the Battalion left COIGN marched here via COIGNEUX & SAILLY. March was by platoons at 100 yards distance — some distance between vehicles from SAILLY onwards. The leading platoon was met at SAILLY church at 5 pm by a staff officer of the 145th Brigade to which the Battalion is attached to for training in the trenches. The night was dark & the roads very heavy. No activity in front of the enemy. Units of the Battalion are distributed as follows — Hd Qrs & A Coy attached to 4th R. Berks. Regt. B " " " Bucks Bn Oxford & Bucks L.I. C " " " 5th Gloucestershire Regt. D " " " 4th Oxford & Bucks L.I. Transport was based on SAILLY.	
	" 28		The general scheme of instruction to be carried out is as follows — Each platoon is attached to one Company of the Battn. to which its (the platoon's) Coy is attached — see above. Each platoon is to man the two 2 Support Trenches for 24 hours under instruction of Officers & Units to which they are attached. Both Platoons & Coys are to hold trenches under their own officers for periods of 24 hours.	

Army Form C. 2118.

WAR DIARY
or
INTELLIGENCE SUMMARY. 10th R. Innskilling Fusiliers
(Erase heading not required.)

Instructions regarding War Diaries and Intelligence Summaries are contained in F. S. Regs., Part II. and the Staff Manual respectively. Title pages will be prepared in manuscript.

Place	Date 1915	Hour	Summary of Events and Information	Remarks and references to Appendices
HEBUTERNE	Oct 28		Each unit of the Battalion takes all orders from the unit to which it is attached. Each number of Hd Qrs receives instruction from the corresponding officer of the 4th R. Berks Regt. The village has been greatly damaged by shell fire – according to report this was occasioned mainly by the French who took the village from the Germans earlier in the year. Recent rains have made the roads very heavy. Trenches are in good order but already the drainage requires incessant attention.	
	Nov 1		Orders for march to COLIN tomorrow have been received from Hd Qrs 145th Brigade by all units of the Battn, through units to which they are attached. All ranks specially mention the very great assistance given in all forms of instruction by the officers, N.C.O's & men of the units amongst which the Battalion has been distributed. Relations have been throughout of the very best. Following is cited as one of many instances – without exception opposite numbers of the 145th Brigade shared their rum with our men. "Rum issue for members of this Battn went astray – without exception opposite numbers of the 145th Brigade shared their rum with our men." Weather for last two days has been wet, but mild.	

1577 Wt. W10791/1773 500,000 1/15 D. D. & L. A.D.S.S./Forms/C. 2118.

Army Form C. 2118.

WAR DIARY
or
INTELLIGENCE SUMMARY.   10th R. Inniskilling Fusiliers

(Erase heading not required.)

Instructions regarding War Diaries and Intelligence Summaries are contained in F. S. Regs., Part II. and the Staff Manual respectively. Title pages will be prepared in manuscript.

Place	Date 1915	Hour	Summary of Events and Information	Remarks and references to Appendices
COUIN	Nov 2		Battalion marched here today via SAILLY & COIGNEUX. Trenches were vacated by Platoons which went back to SAILLY by communication trench from HEBUTERNE & thence to COUIN by road. Enemy opened burst of M.G. & Shell fire on communication trench & road to SAILLY, but caused no casualty. All units under canvas here by 1 p.m. Heavy sufficient enough Casualty return for period of instruction is nil. Heavy rain until dusk.	
	3		Attached for the day to 144th Brigade. Orders received to march tomorrow to BEAUVAL, renewing here under Canvas for this night.	
BEAUVAL	4		Battalion marched here from COUIN at 8.30 am reached billets here at 12.30 p.m. Roads very heavy but weather bright & fine. Lieut J.M. McCleane evacuated. Work on Rifle Range commenced.	
	5		Route march: 4 Coys proceeded by different routes to point of assembly, march time well worked out by Coy Commanders	

1577 Wt.W10791/1773 500,000 1/15 D. D. & L.   A.D.S.S./Forms/C. 2118.

Army Form C. 2118.

WAR DIARY
or
INTELLIGENCE SUMMARY.
(Erase heading not required.)

10th R. Inniskilling Fusiliers

Instructions regarding War Diaries and Intelligence Summaries are contained in F. S. Regs., Part II. and the Staff Manual respectively. Title pages will be prepared in manuscript.

Place	Date 1915	Hour	Summary of Events and Information	Remarks and references to Appendices
BEAUVAL	Nov 10		Night march to Brigade Rendezvous. Time worked out fairly well in spite of heavy roads.	
	13		Following is extract from Report on Battalion, whilst at HEBUTERNE, by G.O.C. 145th Brigade –	
			" The Brigadier is very pleased with the result.	
			(1) " The G.O.C. 145th Brigade reports that the discipline & state of efficiency of the battalion is judged during the attachment from 25th Oct till 1st Nov are in every way satisfactory."	
			(2) " The 10th Battn. R. Innis. Fus. was marching well when seen by the G.O.C. 145th Brigade, & appear to be a good battalion.	
			(3) " They have been entered to shell fire."	
			(4) " The behaviour of the battalion has been good, their camp was kept in a good & sanitary condition."	Struck twice
			Rifle Range completed – 35 yards, 4 pits for men working disappearing targets	
	14		Steady snow fall.	
	15		March by day to Brigade Rendezvous. Owing to bad state of roads the Transport was not taken. Timing worked out very accurately.	
	17		Re-inoculation commenced – my platoons in rotation	
	18		Thaw & rain set in. Roads very heavy. Rifle Range damaged by slides	

1577 Wt.W10791/1773 500,000 1/15 D.D.&L. A.D.S.S./Forms/C. 2118.

Army Form C. 2118.

WAR DIARY
or
INTELLIGENCE SUMMARY.

10th R. Inniskilling Fus.

(Erase heading not required.)

Place	Date 1915	Hour	Summary of Events and Information	Remarks and references to Appendices
BEAUVAL	Mar 24. 26		All officers attended a lecture on F.G.C.M. by the Brigade Major. Orders received for change of quarters to GORENFLOS.	
GORENFLOS	27		Battalion left BEAUVAL at 8.15 am today, arriving at billets here at 1.30 pm. Weather was fine, roads in poor order, marching was handicapped by recent issue of a large number of new boots which, owing to delay in receipt by this Btn, the men had not time to get into proper condition. Billets for men found to be on the whole better than at BEAUVAL but accommodation for officers is very limited. Brigade Hd Qrs & 1 Coy 2nd Essex Regt also billeted in this village. Units which vacated these billets here 2 days ago left everything in filthy condition. No traces of latrines or incinerators - gardens, paths & even rooms have been used for these purposes. Work on latrines & incinerators began at once - special fatigue parties to clean up billets generally.	officers billets
	28		Work on billets continued. Very bad frost.	

1577 Wt.W10791/1773 500,000 1/15 D.D.&L.   A.D.S.S./Forms/C. 2118.

16 & R. Innsbk? Jan 3   Vol 23 -
                        6 Dec 31
                         171
                        7910

36 Kw

WAR DIARY
or
INTELLIGENCE SUMMARY.
(Erase heading not required.)

Army Form C. 2118.

10th R. Inniskilling Fusiliers

Place	Date 1915	Hour	Summary of Events and Information	Remarks and references to Appendices
GORENFLOS	Nov 29		Work on billets continued. Road sweeper obtained & used. Mud paths constructed & road drainage cleared.	7FD
	30		do	7FD
	Dec 3		Work also begun on field ovens. Continued rain showers. Divisional Tactical Exercise fixed for today, cancelled owing to continuous rain. Again postponed owing to bad weather.	7FD
	7		" " again postponed	7FD
	8		Roads, other than first class roads, in bad state. Open country very heavy. A ½ Battalion route march constructed. Each of the 2 bath houses capable of bathing 2 Coys in 3 days.	7FD
	15		Machine Gun Section took part in Brigade Practice of indirect fire. Signalling officer with 2 telephones in co-operation. Result is reported as good.	7FD
	17		Pace of march altered from 120 to 112 per minute. Weather continues bad. Frequent showers.	(7FD)
	18		"Closing of gates of Londonderry 1688, 18 Dec. 1688" celebrated with usual honours.	7FD

Army Form C. 2118.

WAR DIARY
or
INTELLIGENCE SUMMARY.
(Erase heading not required.)

10th R. Innishilling Fusiliers

Instructions regarding War Diaries and Intelligence Summaries are contained in F. S. Regs., Part II. and the Staff Manual respectively. Title pages will be prepared in manuscript.

Place	Date 19/15	Hour	Summary of Events and Information	Remarks and references to Appendices
GOIRENZOS	19 Dec 19	11.1 pm	Information received through Brigade HQrs of 2 Zeppelins, 1 going NW from YPRES at 8 pm, 1 going S from POPERINGHE at 8.20 pm.	7D
		11.15 pm	1 airship reported going S. over ST. RIQUIER. None of the above were seen by this Battn. Night was clear with moonlight.	7D
	20		In accordance with memo from Div. Hdqrs, heavy training is stopped at 12.30 pm each day. Association Football matches in top league system commenced today; to be continued & matches each afternoon.	7D
	21		Weather continues wet - incessant rain showers.	7D
	22		Capt. Waring Smyth admitted to Field Ambulance with acute bronchitis, evacuated this same day to Cas. Clearing station.	7D
	24		Draft of 9 / Corporals + 22 men arrived at 7 am from Base, to replace sick wastage. Two men reported by the conducting officer as having deserted en route at ROUEN.	7D
			2/Lieut. A. Spalding reported for duty at 2.30 pm.	
	25		Christmas Day - Holiday. 2 absentees from Draft reported here, bringing number of Draft up to 25 other ranks. Weather finer, very little rain.	89D
	27		Boxing Day - Holiday. No rain - mild. Lt Col. Ross Smyth, C.O. proceeded on leave. Major G. H. Smith (2nd in C) taking over command of the Battalion.	Without delay 7D

1577 Wt.W10791/1773 500,000 1/15 D.D. & L. A.D.S.S./Forms/C. 2118.

Army Form C. 2118.

WAR DIARY
or
INTELLIGENCE SUMMARY.

10th R. Inniskilling Fusiliers

(Erase heading not required.)

Place	Date 1915	Hour	Summary of Events and Information	Remarks and references to Appendices
GORENFLOS	29 Dec		C.O. warned of probable move next week.	751
	30		Orders received for 2 Coys to proceed tomorrow to GEZAINCOURT. Remainder of Battalion warned for readiness to move on or about 5th Jan/16. Weather fine but turning colder.	751
	31		A & B Coys under Major Murray proceeded to GEZAINCOURT with all stores, spare kit etc of the Detachment.	751

LB. 3.
6 sheets

B6

To the R. Russell ? Ros.
Vol. 4.

Army Form C. 2118.

WAR DIARY
or
INTELLIGENCE SUMMARY: 10 I.R. Inniskilling Fusiliers
(Erase heading not required.)

Place	Date 1916	Hour	Summary of Events and Information	Remarks and references to Appendices
GORENFLOS	Jan 1		Orders received for move to BONNEVILLE on 6th inst. Billeting party of 1 officer, 1 French interpreter & 4 other ranks proceeded in advance to take over billets from 16th Batt. Manchester Regt.	
	2		Draft of 24 other ranks arrived today from Base — one man is reported as missing en route. Very high wind from W — some showers. Temperature mild	77D
			Absentee from Draft reported present, bringing total of Draft to 25 other ranks	77D
	4		Practice of Brigade attack in 3 lines of trenches. Ground very heavy & trenches wet. Practice reported as being well carried out.	77D3
	5		1 Platoon of D Coy (Strength 1 officer & 41 other ranks) proceeded to DOULLENS to report for duty to Hd. Qrs. 14th Corps.	77D3
BONNEVILLE	6		Battalion (less 9 Platoons) marched from GORENFLOS at 8.15 a.m. & proceeded to billets here via DOMART, BERNEUIL & MONTRELET. Roads were very heavy & goodness knows shipping for transport vehicles. Troops in billets at 12.40 pm. Billeting accommodation here is very indifferent — Barns & houses are in bad state of repair. Outgoing units left a few latrines & one or two very poor incinerators	

WAR DIARY
or
INTELLIGENCE SUMMARY
(Erase heading not required.)

Army Form C. 2118.

10th R. Innis. Fusiliers

Place	Date 1916	Hour	Summary of Events and Information	Remarks and references to Appendices
BONNEVILLE	Jan 6		No field orders appear to have been constructed. Village stands in heavy clay & is in very muddy state.	7aD
	" 7		Work in billets commenced yesterday, continued today. Lt Col ROSS SMYTH & Capt E.H. BARTON returned from leave – former resumes command of the Battalion. Frequent rain showers moved.	7aD
	" 8		Draft of 25 other Ranks which joined on 1st inst, proceeded today to GEZAINCOURT for duty with A Coy to which they had been posted, having been retained with remainder of the Battalion pending yesterday's move. Lt H. ALLOM proceeded on leave.	7aD
	" 9		Weather cold & fine. 14th Div Arty report by wire that two Zeppelins were seen south of YPRES at 3.30 pm travelling East.	7aD
	" 11		D. Coy (less No 15 Platoon, & Band + members of Battn Bomb class) marched today to DOULLENS for duty with 150th F. Coy R.E. Present distribution of the Battalion is as follows :– { Battn Hd Qrs, Band, + Battn Bombers, } { Machine Gun Sect + Transport (Kers 2 } — BONNEVILLE. { C. Coy. (Lim Wagons) } A + B Coy, 2 limbered wagons + 2 drivers .... GEZAINCOURT. D Coy .... DOULLENS Rear Party 2 N.C.Os & 8 men under Page officers .... GORENFLOS.	7aD

Army Form C. 2118.

WAR DIARY
or
INTELLIGENCE SUMMARY.

(Erase heading not required.)

10th R. Innskilling Fusiliers

Instructions regarding War Diaries and Intelligence Summaries are contained in F.S. Regs., Part II. and the Staff Manual respectively. Title pages will be prepared in manuscript.

Place	Date 1916	Hour	Summary of Events and Information	Remarks and references to Appendices
BONNEVILLE	Jun 12		Lieut R. SHAW proceeded on leave. Capt T.E. MILLER & Servant proceeded today to ENGLEBELMER for 1 months instruction with 2nd R. Irish Regt.	70/3 70/0
	19		Lieut H.M. ALLEN returned from leave	
	22		Lieut Wakley Lieut A.W. WAKLEY & 2 Lieut W.R. GAUSSEN & with 33 other Ranks of the Vickers Machine Gun Section proceeded to Brigade Head Qrs tomorrow 23rd inst for duty with new M.G. Coy. They will ultimately be struck off the strength of the Battalion. 2nd Lieut G.E. AUSTIN appointed Battn Lewis machine Gun officer — Formation training of the new M.G. Section commenced today. Battn Musketry classes, for approximately 50 NCOs & men per class, commenced today. All NCOs men & last 2 drafts from this present Class. Each Class lasts 4 days.	
	23 24		Lieut A-SPO R SHAW returned from leave.	70/0
	24		At 10.45 pm fire broke out in a large barn in the French billets of this village. All details here were turned out & the fire was extinguished at 5.30 am on 25th inst.	70/0
	26		Three Officers & 4 N.C.Os despatched to Divisional School of Instruction commencing today.	70/0

Army Form C. 2118.

WAR DIARY
or
INTELLIGENCE SUMMARY.

10th R. Innoskilling Fus.

(Erase heading not required.)

Place	Date 1916	Hour	Summary of Events and Information	Remarks and references to Appendices
BONNEVILLE	Jan 29		2 Lieut G.H. GIBSON reported for duty on joining & taken on the strength.	750
	30		Major G.H. BRUSH (2nd in command) proceeded to Lt. Col. MAILLARD to take up duties of commandant at 36th Divisional School of Instruction	7523
	31		With an Hutments cound. Programme for Tactical training & Route marching laid down for this week. Major F.S.N. MACRORY proceed on leave	750

1577 Wt. W10791/1773 500,000 1/15 D. D. & L. A.D.S.S./Forms/C. 2118.

WAR DIARY or INTELLIGENCE SUMMARY.

Army Form C. 2118.

10th R. Innesskilling Fusiliers

(Erase heading not required.)

Place	Date 1916	Hour	Summary of Events and Information	Remarks and references to Appendices
BONNEVILLE	Feby 1		Information received from Brigade Hd Qrs that all detached units of the Battn will rejoin at Battn Hd Qrs here in course of the next three days.	7DD
	2		Orders received for transfer of most of the Division into the XVII Corps & for move this week into a portion of the line lately the allotted to the XVII Corps.	7DD
			The Battalion marches from Billets here on 5th inst.	
			Lieut C.N.L. STRONGE proceeded on leave. D. Coy less 1 Platoon rejoined at 4 pm from DOULLENS. A & B Coys rejoined at 11 pm from GEZAINCOURT.	7DD
	3		No 15 Platoon (D Coy) rejoined from DOMART.	7DD
	5		Lieut C.N.L. STRONGE proceeded from leave. Battalion marched at 8.50 am from BONNEVILLE & reached billets here at 1 pm. Day was fine and normal. Recent rains had made the roads very heavy.	7DD
TOUTENCOURT ACHEUX	6		Battalion marched from TOUTENCOURT at 8.50 am under orders to go into billets at FORCEVILLE. When at west outskirts of VARENNES orders were received changing billets to ACHEUX. Billets here were reached at 11 am. Duties of the Battalion are to assist R.E. in railway construction.	7DD

Army Form C. 2118.

WAR DIARY
or
INTELLIGENCE SUMMARY.   10th R. Innis. Fus.
(Erase heading not required.)

Instructions regarding War Diaries and Intelligence Summaries are contained in F. S. Regs., Part II. and the Staff Manual respectively. Title pages will be prepared in manuscript.

Place	Date 1916	Hour	Summary of Events and Information	Remarks and references to Appendices
ACHEUX	Feb 7		3 officers + 500 other ranks detailed for duty with 109th Railway Coy. R.E. for work on construction of railway line. Battalion has also to furnish H.Q. as Grand & fatigue parties to Town Commandant. Billets are indifferent & very muddy. Transport lines are deep in mud & with tent accommodation for the men.	750
	8		Capt J.T.E. MILLER rejoined from attachment and to 2nd R. Irish Regt.	750
	9		Slight fall of snow between 6 & 8 am. Remainder of day bright & fine. Q.M.S. COX & Sergeant 2/Lieut dated 30.1.16 — Taken on strength of officers.	750
	11		Captains R.S. KNOX & J.C.B. PROCTOR proceeded on leave as from 10 Z inst. Major F.S.M. MACRORY reported, on leaving returned from leave.	ditto
	12		Detachment of A & B Coys. under the Command of Major F.S.M. MACRORY (together with 1 Lewis machine gun and one gun team, consisting of Captain. M. Rowlo. ROBERTSON. 2/Lieut. G.E. AUSTIN. 2/Lieut. K.A. MACKENZIE, 2/Lieut. A.N. NESBITT and 196 other ranks. Proceeded via MAILLY-MAILLET. to the trenches for 4 days instruction with the 15th R. IRISH. RIFLES. Two platoons with 2 officers of the 15th R. IRISH RIFLES arrived and are attached to 'B' Coy. for 4 days, occupying billets vacated by French detachment. etc	ditto

ACHEUX

WAR DIARY or INTELLIGENCE SUMMARY

Army Form C. 2118.

10th R. Innis. Fus.

(Erase heading not required.)

Place	Date 1916	Hour	Summary of Events and Information	Remarks and references to Appendices
ACHEUX	Feb. 12		A draft of 29 men reported today having travelled from near YPRES where they had been attached to the 1st Entrenching Batt^n (2nd Canadian Div.) proceeded on leave as from the 11th inst.	apx
			CAPT^N J.T.E. MILLER proceeded to the 3rd Army School of Instruction, FLIXECOURT	apx
	14		Captn & Adjutant F.D. BOYD proceeded to the 3rd Army School of Instruction, FLIXECOURT on a 1 months Special Course for Adjutants. CAPT^N A.F. COOK will act as Adjutant during Captain BOYD's absence.	apx
	16		2 Platoons of 'C' Coy under the command of Captain. E.H. BARTON, accompanied by 2/Lieut Chillingworth proceeded to the trenches at AUCHON VILLERS for instruction with the 9th Bn. R. IRISH RIFLES. They marched out 104 all ranks. The 9th Bn. R. IRISH RIFLES sent 2 Platoons to be attached to us in their place. 2/Lieut. J.W. SHANNON and 2/Lieut J. ALLEN reported having joined from draft and have posted to B + A Coys respectively. Captain M.A. ROBERTSON. Proceeded on leave under date of 18th inst. Major BRUSH having been appointed Commandant of the 36th Div. School of Instruction. Major F.S.N. MACRORY has been appointed acting Second-in-command during his absence.	apx apx apx apx apx
	19			
	20.		No 21660 Pte. MUNDELL. D was killed in Action. This is our first Casualty.	apx

WAR DIARY
or
INTELLIGENCE SUMMARY. 10th Bn. R. Innis. Fus.

Army Form C. 2118.

(Erase heading not required.)

Place	Date	Hour	Summary of Events and Information	Remarks and references to Appendices
ACHEUX	Feb. 20th		2 Platoons of "D" Coy under the command of Capt. R.S. KNOX accompanied by 2/Lieut. F. CRAWLEY & 2/Lieut. G.H. GIBSON, proceeded to the trenches at AVELUY VILLERS, for 2 days instruction with the 15th R. IRISH RIFLES.	ats
	21st		2 Platoons of the 15th R. IRISH RIFLES will be attached to us for 2 days up to this date from the 7th inst. we have been supplying daily a party of 400/500 men to assist the R.E's in railway construction at ACHEUX and LEALVILLERS.	ats
TRENCHES	24th		At H.H. 5 p.m. the Batts under the Command of Lt. Col. Ross SMYTH Marched from the 15th R. IRISH RIFLES. ACHEUX to MAILLY to take over trenches from the 15th R. IRISH RIFLES. The Relief was completed at 12.5 midnight with no casualties. During the morning it started to snow and continued until the evening	ats
	25		of the 26th. During the day & night a great number of Rifle Grenades and Trench mortars fell into our Sector especially on a Post known as "The REDAN."	ats
	26		This morning L/Cpl. M. Guire. D. No 15856 was killed by a rifle Grenade at "SUICIDE CORNER." Lieut. Col. Ross SMYTH, left for 3rd Army School of Instruction, FLIXECOURT on a Special ons weeks Course for Commanding Officers	ats

Army Form C. 2118.

WAR DIARY
or
INTELLIGENCE SUMMARY. 10th Bn. R. Innis. Fus

(Erase heading not required.)

Place	Date	Hour	Summary of Events and Information	Remarks and references to Appendices
ACHEUX	July 28		The Battn. was relieved of their tour of the trenches by the 11th Bn. Royal Inniskilling Fusiliers. The relief being completed at 9:55 P.M. As each Coy. was relieved they proceeded into billets at FORCEVILLE where the Battn. is in Divisional Reserve.	over
FORCEVILLE	29		2/Lieut G.H. PLOWMAN (4th Inniskillings) reported his arrival and taken on the strength. 2/Lieut A.W. WAKLEY and 2/Lieut W.A. GAUSSEN appeared in this days orders as having been transferred to the 109th Machine Gun Company and were accordingly struck off the strength.	over over

XXXVI 10 Inniskilly Fy 6 Vol 4 5. φ 7 mths

Confidential

War Diary

of

10th (S) Bn. Royal Inniskilling Fus,

from

1st to 31st March 1916.
(Volume 6)

Officer i/c A.G's Office
Base.

WAR DIARY 10th B. R. Innis. Fus.

Army Form C. 2118.

Place	Date	Hour	Summary of Events and Information	Remarks and references to Appendices
ACHEUX	March 2nd 1916		Orders were received this evening for the Battn to move tomorrow to MARTINSART to take over part of the line held by units of the 146th and 147th Brigade.	Ap
MARTINSART	3/4		At 10.30 A.M. the Battn moved out of FORCEVILLE Commanded by Major MAERSRY and arrived via HEDAUVILLE and ENGLEBELMER at MARTINSART at 1-15 P.M. The Battn went into billets in the night and came under the orders of the 146th + 147th Brigades. A + B Coys under 146th and C + D Coys under 147th. During the night of 3/4 March there was a heavy snow fall.	Ap
"	5.		Lt Col Ross Smyth rejoined from FLIXECOURT. A & B Coys under the Command of Captain M. ROBERTSON departed for AUTHUILLE to take over the defences there. A draft of 30 N.C.O.'s + men joined on this day.	Ap Ap
"	6.		On this day the Battn Comdr. made over the command of the 109th Brigade 2/Lieut. CRAWLEY took over the Garrison of he halons and the Mill Pool at AUTHUILLE.	Ap Ap
MARTINSART	7.		One platoon of a section of 10 Coy. relieved the Garrison of he halons and kept one with drawn the 11th R. IRISH RIFLES. This Garrison at he halons post was withdrawn taking over the duties	Ap Ap

Army Form C. 2118.

WAR DIARY
or
INTELLIGENCE SUMMARY.   10th Bn. R. Innis. Fus.
(Erase heading not required.)

Place	Date	Hour	Summary of Events and Information	Remarks and references to Appendices
TRENCHES	March 1916 8th		Orders were received for the Battn. to relieve the 9th Bn. R. Innis. Fus. on the night of the 9th in the trenches at THIEPVAL Wood.	att
	9th		The Battn. relieved the 9th Bn. R. Innis. Fus. relief being completed at 10 p.m.	att
	10th		The night of 9/10th and the day of 10th was fairly quiet, but 2/Cpl Boraid "B" Coy was killed by a trench mortar.	att
	11th		About 11 p.m. the enemy opened a very heavy bombardment which lasted until about 1.30 A.M. 11th inst. They however did not attack. A great deal of damage was done to our wire, our front line and outpost trenches. We lost 4 killed and 10 wounded.	att
	12th		In the trenches	
MARTINSART	13th		The Battn. was relieved by the 9th Bn. R. Innis Fus. relief being completed at 9.10. P.M. After relief A & B Coys with Headquarters proceeded to rest billets at MARTINSART. "C" Coy to garrison GORDON CASTLE and JOHNSTONES POST. "D" Coy to garrison AUTHUILLE. Captain and Adjutant F.D. BOYD rejoined this evening and resumed his duties as Adjutant	att att

WAR DIARY
or
INTELLIGENCE SUMMARY.
(Erase heading not required.)

Army Form C. 2118.

Place	Date	Hour	Summary of Events and Information	Remarks and references to Appendices
	March 16.		Captain t. S. Rough, having been appointed Commandant 36th Div. School of Instruction, BEAUVAL, the duties of adjutant were again taken over by Captain A. F. Cook. The following is an extract from a "Special order of the day" issued by the G.O.C. 36th Division with reference to the Bombardment night of 10th/11th inst.	
			"Special order of the day" By Major-General O.S.N. NUGENT. D.S.O. Commanding. 36th (ULSTER) Division.	
			The Divisional Commander has now received reports on the nature of the German Bombardment on the trenches held by the 10TH ROYAL INNISKILLING FUSILIERS under Command of Lieut-Col. ROSS SMYTH on the night of 10th/11th March. There seems no reason to doubt that the German Bombardment was intended to cover a raid on our lines similar to the raid which actually took place elsewhere the same night. The Divisional Commander has read with great satisfaction	

WAR DIARY or INTELLIGENCE SUMMARY

Army Form C. 2118.

Place	Date	Hour	Summary of Events and Information	Remarks and references to Appendices
MARTINSART TRENCHES	March 19.		of the Sheikhinois with which the 10th ROYAL INNISKILLING. FUSILIERS, kept up a steady fire from their trenches throughout the bombardment and of their coolness and gallantry. (Signed) R.C. SINGLETON. MAJOR D.A.A & Q.M.G. 36th Division	a/c
	24.		14th March 1916. The Battn relieved the 9th Bn. R. Innis. Fus in the trenches this evening. Lieut. E. McCLURE proceeded on leave.	a/c
	25.		The 9th Bn. R. Innis. Fus relieved us the night of 25th inst. on completion of the relief C & D Coys returned to billets in MARTINSART. "A" Coy garrisoning AUTHVILLE, "B" Coy garrisoning GORDON CASTLE and JOHNSON'S POST	a/c
MARTINSART			MAJOR. G.H. BRUSH having returned from the 36th Div. School of instruction resumed his duties as Second-in-Command	a/c
	26		"A" & "B" Coys were relieved this evening by 2 Coys of 11th Bn. ROYAL IRISH RIFLES. and went into billets at MARTINSART.	a/c

WAR DIARY
or
INTELLIGENCE SUMMARY.

(Erase heading not required.)

Army Form C. 2118.

10th Bn. R. Innis. Fus.

Place	Date	Hour	Summary of Events and Information	Remarks and references to Appendices
	March 31.		The Battalion relieved the 9th Bn. R. Innis. Fus. in the trenches THIEPVAL WOOD this evening.	A12

War Diary.

10th (S) Bn. R. Innis Fusrs

From 1st. April 1916   To. 30th. April 1916.

Army Form C. 2118

WAR DIARY
or
INTELLIGENCE SUMMARY

(Erase heading not required.)

1st Bn. R. Inniskilling Fusiliers

Place	Date	Hour	Summary of Events and Information	Remarks and references to Appendices
THIEPVAL WOOD	April 1916 1/6		Major G. H. BRUSH proceeded on leave this evening. In the trenches in Section G.2. THIEPVAL WOOD. A very quiet time having only 1 casualty killed viz. No. 15218 Sgt. Black D of 'A' Coy. The Battalion was relieved on the night of the 6th inst. by the 9th Bn. R. Innis. Fus. During the relief the enemy raided trenches just N. of THIEPVAL WOOD (36th Division) some of the shells coming into our sector, which delayed the relief, causing however no casualties. The Battalion went into billets at MARTINSART.	ap ap
MARTINSART	8/11		The Battalion provided working parties of about 300 men daily for the 121st & 150th Coys. R.E. most of them working in the front line and support trenches. Captain A. F. COOK proceeded on leave.	ap
	10		Lt. Col. Ross Smyth proceeded on leave. The Command of the Battn. was taken over by Major. J.S.M. MACRORY.	ap
	12		The Battn. relieved the 9th Bn. R. Innis. Fus. in the trenches this evening in Section G.2. THIEPVAL WOOD	ap
THIEPVAL WOOD	15		Major G.H. BRUSH having returned from leave took over command	ap

Army Form C. 2118

WAR DIARY
or
INTELLIGENCE SUMMARY
(Erase heading not required.)

10th Bn. R. Inniskilling Fusiliers

Instructions regarding War Diaries and Intelligence Summaries are contained in F.S. Regs., Part II. and the Staff Manual respectively. Title Pages will be prepared in manuscript.

Place	Date	Hour	Summary of Events and Information	Remarks and references to Appendices
THIEPVAL WOOD	April 1916 17.		The Battn. was relieved by the 9th Bn. R. Innis. Fus. this evening and proceeded to billets in MARTINSART. During this tour the Battn. had a very quiet time having 1 casualty killed only, viz, No 15556 Pte. Graham W. 'B' Coy.	atc
	18		Lt. Col. Ross Smyth and Captain A.F. Cook returned from leave, having been recalled. This meant was general throughout the Army. The Battn. found working parties under the 155th Coy. R.E.'s of about two hrs daily.	atc
	19/23		This evening a raid on the Enemy's trenches. from the right of THIEPVAL WOOD, was carried out by the 32nd Div. Our artillery from Bouzard for about 1 hour from 9.30 p.m. to 10.30 p.m. And as retaliation was expected by a bombardment of MARTINSART, the Battn. stood ready to proceed to cellars, funk holes, trenches etc. The Enemy did not however retaliate on MARTINSART.	atc
MARTINSART	22			atc
	23		Lieut. C.N.L. STRONGE proceeded today to the 4th Army School of Instruction, FLIXECOURT for a months General Course.	atc
	24		Easter Monday. Treated as a holiday	atc

WAR DIARY or **INTELLIGENCE SUMMARY**

1st Bn. R. Inniskilling Fusiliers

Army Form C. 2118

Place	Date	Hour	Summary of Events and Information	Remarks and references to Appendices
THIEPVAL	April 1916 25.		The usual working patrol of about two men were found.	A2
	26		The following officers reported and were taken on the Strength. 2/Lieut. J.L. RITTER. 2/Lieut. A. KEMP. 2/Lieut. J.M. MONTGOMERY 2/Lieut. F.W. DAVIDSON. The first 3 have already served in the Battalion previous to our proceeding to FRANCE. Captain E.H. BARTON. 2/Lieut. J.W. DRENNAN. 2/Lieut. K.A. McKENZIE proceeded home on leave & draft of 16 reported on this date and were taken on the Strength.	A2 A2
	28.		2/Lieut. J. DOUGLAS proceeded to the BASE for duty in training drafts etc. He will remain there for a period of 2 months.	A2
	30.		A Coy + B Coy proceeded to day to relieve 2 Coys of the 1st R Irish Rifles. A Coy to South Antrim Villas in THIEPVAL. B Coy to AVELUY. They will act as Supporting Companies to the 11th R. Irish Rifles who hold the line in THIEPVAL WOOD	A2

S E C R E T.

Reference Map Sheet No 57D.
1/40,000

Copy No. 6

Battalion
~~Operation~~ Order No. 10.
by
LIEUT-COL. W. F. Hessey,
Commanding, 11th (S) Bn. Rl. Inniskilling Fus.
2nd April, 1916.

1. The 109th Brigade will take over portion of the line now held by the 92nd Brigade on the evening of the 2nd/3rd April.

2. The 11th Bn. Rl. Inniskilling Fusiliers will be relieved by the 14th Bn. Royal Irish Rifles in the trenches on the night of 2nd/3rd April.
   The 14th Bn. Royal Irish Rifles in addition to the front now held by the 11th Bn. Rl. Inniskilling Fusiliers will also take over from 13th Battn. East Yorks of 92nd Infantry Brigade the portion of the front extending from junction of Q.17.6. and Q.17.7. to the junction of Q.17.11 and Q.17.12.
   The 11th Bn. Rl. Inniskilling Fusiliers will take over the posts and billets now occupied by the 14th Bn. Royal Irish Rifles.

3. The order in which Companies will be relieved will be as follows:-
   1st. Reserve Company.   Our "A" Coy. by "C" Coy. 14th R.Ir.R.
   2nd. Right Front   "   "   "D" "   " "B" "   -"-
   3rd. Left Front   "   "   "B" "   " "D" "   -"-
   4th Support   "   "   "C" "   " "A" "   -"-

4. O.C. "D" Coy. will arange to take over posts at MOUND KEEP - McMAHONS POST - and - AVELUY WOOD by 5.30 p.m.
   O.C. "C" Coy. will arrange to reinforce "D" Coy. with necessary support to enable this party to be withdrawn.

5. Guides for relieving Companies will be at the junction of MESNIL - HAMEL ROAD, south of village at 7.15 p.m.

6. All trench stores will be handed over and lists sent in to Adjutant on 3rd April by 12 noon.
   Billets and Posts will be taken from the 14th Bn. Royal Irish Rifles as early as possible on evening of 2nd April by representatives who will withdraw via JACOBS LADDER.

7. Each Company will hand over to their relief a table showing the work in hand.

8. On completion of relief O.C. Companies will report by RUNNER to Headquarters in trenches.

(Sd) W. Moore Capt.,
Adjt. 11th (S) Bn. Rl. Inniskilling Fusiliers.

Issued at................
Copy No. 1 ....
 "   "   2 ....
 "   "   3 ....
 "   "   4 ....
 "   "   5 ....
 "   "   6 14TH R. IRISH RIFLES
 "   "   7 ....

S E C R E T.

Reference Map, Sheet No. 57d,   Copy No. 1
   1/40,000.

BATTALION ORDER No. 11.
by
LIEUT. COLONEL W. F. HESSEY
COMMANDING, 11th.(S)Bn.Rl.Inniskilling Fus.
8th. April, 1916.

1.   The Battalion will relieve the 14th. Rl. Irish Rifles in the Trenches on the night of 8th/9th. April.
      The 14th. Rl. Irish Rifles will take over the posts & billets of the 11th. Rl. Inniskilling Fusiliers on relief.

2.   Order in which Companies will be relieved will be as follows,:-

      1st. Reserve Coy.   Our "D" Coy. relieve "C" Coy. 14th.
      2nd. Right   "   "A" "   "   "B" "   Royal
      3rd. Left   "   "B" "   "   "D" "   Irish
      4th. Centre   "   "C" "   "   "A" "   Rifles.

      "D" Company will enter HAMEL at 7.30 p.m. from MOUND KEEP.
      "A" Company start from the Barrier at 7.35 p.m., followed by "B" and "C" Companies at 200 yards intervals between Companies and Platoons, in single file.
      Guides from 14th. Rl. Irish Rifles will meet Companies at the entrance to HAMEL.

3.   Each Company will send one Officer and 2 N.C.O's to take over Trench Stores etc., to arrive in Trenches not later than 4 p.m.

      Representatives of each Company to be left behind to hand over Billets.

      Signallers, etc., to arrive in Trenches not later than 4 p.m.

4.   The Guards in HAMEL will be found by "C" Company and will be reduced to 3 men per Guard.

5.   Each Company will arrange to take over the work in hand.

6.   Completion of Relief will be reported to Headquarters in Trenches by Runners and by telephone message.

                                    (Sd) W. Moore, Captain.
                     Adjt, 11th.(S)Bn.Rl.Inniskilling Fusrs.

Issued at 10 a.m.

     Copy No. 1. 14th Rl Irish Rifles
     "   2.
     "   3.
     "   4.
     "   5.
     "   6.
     "   7.

SECRET.

Copy No. 2

Reference Map, Sheet No. 57G.
1/40,000.

BATTALION ORDER No. 12.
by
LIEUT. COLONEL, W. F. HESSEY
COMMANDING, 11th. (S)Bn. Rl. INNISKILLING FUSRS.
14.4.16.

1. The 11th. Rl. Innis. Fus. will be relieved by the 14th. Rl. Irish Rifles in the LEFT SUB-SECTOR, on the night of the 14th./15th. April, 1916.

2. Order of reliefs will be as follows:-

    Reserve Coy. Our "D" Coy. will be relieved by "D" Coy. 14th.
    Centre   "   " "C" "   "   "   "   "C" " Royal
    Left   "   " "B" "   "   "   "   "B" " Irish
    Right   "   " "A" "   "   "   "   "A" " Rifles.

3. Guides will meet relieving Companies at the Battalion Dump at 7.30 p.m.

4. Representatives of 14th. Rl. Irish Rifles will take over Stores from Companies in the afternoon.
    Representatives of our "A" Company, will take over in advance in MOUND KEEP, McMAHON'S POST and AVELUY WOOD, from "A" Company, 14th. Rl. Irish Rifles, with sufficient N.C.O's and men to take over the Guards and Posts, by 6 p.m.

5. Representatives of "B", "C" and "D" Companies, will take over from 14th. Rl. Irish Rifles in MESNIL in afternoon.

6. "D" Company will send up 4 N.C.O's and 12 men to take over the Guards, i.e., 3 men per Guard, at MESNIL by 7 p.m. The remainder of Guards will be mounted later.

7. Lists of all Trench Stores handed over, and all Billet Stores taken over from 14th. Rl. Irish Rifles, will be rendered to Orderly Room by 10 a.m., 15th. April.

8. Completion of Reliefs will be reported to Battalion Headquarters in Trenches by Runners.

(Sd) H.C. Gordon, Lieut.
Atg./Adjt, 11th.(S)Bn. Rl. Innis. Fuslrs.

Issued at 10 a.m.

Copy No. 1
 "   " 2 14th Rl Irish Rifles
 "   " 3   "   "   "   "
 "   " 4   "   "   "   "
 "   " 5   "   "   "   "
 "   " 6   "   "   "   "
 "   " 7   "   "   "   "
 "   " 8   "   "   "   "

RELIEF ORDERS
- by -
Lt. Col. Ross Smyth,
Comdg. 10th Bn Royal Innis Fus.

1. "A" Coy will relieve 1 Coy of the 14th. Bn. Royal I. Rifles in SOUTH ANTRIM VILLAS to-morrow the 30th. inst.

2. "B" Coy will relieve 1 Coy of the 14th. Bn. Royal I. Rifles in AUTHUILLE to-morrow the 30th. inst.

3. The relief will be carried out during the day by platoons with ½ hour interval between platoons and 5 minutes interval between sections.

4. A & B Coys will each send to-day one officer to the Coy they are relieving to make arrangements.

5. A & B Coys will send to-morrow morning 1 officer per Coy. and 1. N.C.O. per platoon also the Coy. Sgt. Major to take over.

6. All arrangements to be made between Coys concerned.

7. Coy Signallers and Lewis Machine Gunners to take over by 12 noon to-morrow.

8. Present billets occupied by A & B Coys to be handed over to 2 Coys 11th. Bn. Royal Innis Fus.

9. All trench stores to be taken over and lists sent to Battn. Orderly Room by 12 noon the 1st. prox.

10. Completion of relief to be reported by wire to Bn. Headquarters.

11. All packs, Coy Stores, blankets etc. to be dumped in yard No.23 Billet Rue d'Eglise by 12 noon. A & B Coys to each send a responsible man to take charge until cleared by transport.

12. The Quartermaster will arrange for rations.

13. The Transport Officer will arrange for his waggons (rations) to leave MARTINSART with the transport of the 14th. Royal I. Rifles. "B" Coys rations being dumped in AUTHUILLE. "A" Coys being sent by pack mules to Dump at SOUTH ANTRIM VILLAS.

14. The Transport Officer will arrange to collect the kits etc. dumped at 23 Billet Rue d'Eglise and convey them to the Q.M. Stores at HEDAUVILLE.

(Sgd) A. F. Cook,
Captain & Adjutant.

No. 3

BATTALION ORDERS No. 15,
by
MAJOR THE EARL OF LEITRIM
COMMANDING, 11th.(S)Bn.Rl.INNISKILLING FUS.
29.4.16.

SECRET.
Reference Map, 57d,
1/40,000

1. The Battalion will be relieved in the RIGHT SUB SECTOR by the 14th. RL. IRISH RIFLES, on the night of 30th. April/1st. May, 1916, and move into Rest Billets as follows.

2. Headquarters, "A" and "C" Companies, in huts in MARTINSART WOOD, at present occupied by 14th. ROYAL IRISH RIFLES.
"B" Company, in Tents in MARTINSART WOOD, at present occupied by 10th. Bn. RL. INNIS. FUSRS.
"D" Company, in Billets in MARTINSART occupied by the 10th. Bn.RL.INNIS.FUSRS.

3. Lieut. THORNTON, with Billeting Party of 1 N.C.O. and 1 Private per Company and Headquarters, will report to the Town Major in MARTINSART at 11.00 a.m. on the 30th. instant.

4. Relief of Companies and Reserve Platoons will be in the following order,:-
"A" Company and Reserve Platoon.
"B" Company and Reserve Platoon.
"D" Company,
"C" Company,
Reserve Platoons of "D" and "C" Companies.

5. "A" and "B" Companies will send guides to AUTHUILE and SOUTH ANTRIM VILLAS respectively at times to be arranged between the Officers Commanding Companies.
Both Companies will return to MARTINSART by the lower road together with their Platoons in Reserve.
Officers Commanding "D" and "C" Companies, and Headquarters, will send guides to BLACK HORSE CORNER at 7.00 p.m.

6. Officers Kits will be taken to the Dump by 7.30 p.m.

7. The Transport Officer will arrange to bring up Officers Kits of 14th. Bn.RL. IRISH RIFLES, and the same limbers will return with Officers' Kits.

8. The Quartermaster will make all necessary arrangements with regard to Rations and the exchange of cooking utensils.

9. Officers Horses will be sent to BLACK HORSE CORNER at the following times.:-
"A" Company,   8.00 p.m.
"B"   "   8.00 p.m.
"D"   "   8.30 p.m.
"C"   "   9.00 p.m.
Headquarters,   9.30 p.m.

10. Completion of reliefs will be reported to Battalion Head Quarters in the Trenches by telephone and runners, using the word "TEMPO" and stating the time.

12. Lists of Trench Stores handed over will be rendered to Orderly Room by 12 noon on the 1st. proximo.

Issued at 3.30 p.m.

Copy No. 1. 109th. Bde.
 "   " 2. Comdg. Officer
 "   " 3. 14th.R.I.Rif.
 "   " 4. O.C. "A" Coy.
 "   " 5.   "   "B" "
 "   " 6.   "   "C" "
 "   " 7.   "   "D" "
 "   " 8. Q.Mr.& Tran.Off.
 "   " 9. File.

(Sd) W. Moore, Captain,
Adjt, 11th.(S)Bn.Rl.Inniskilling Fusrs.

10 Inniskilling vol 6

Confidential.

War Diary

of

10th (S) Battn., Royal Inniskilling Fus.

from $1\frac{5}{16}$ to $31\frac{5}{16}$.

The
Officer i/c A.G. Office
Base.

Army Form C. 2118

WAR DIARY
or
INTELLIGENCE SUMMARY
(Erase heading not required.)

10th Bn. R. Inniskilling Fusiliers

Instructions regarding War Diaries and Intelligence Summaries are contained in F.S. Regs., Part II. and the Staff Manual respectively. Title Pages will be prepared in manuscript.

Place	Date	Hour	Summary of Events and Information	Remarks and references to Appendices
A U T H U I L E	May, 1916 1/2		A & B Coys in Support trenches. C & D Coys found working parties of 145 men.	ate
	2		No 15650 L/Cpl Kane W. was wounded in AUTHUILLE and died on the way to hospital. 2/Lieut. T. W. COX proceeded from on special leave. 2/Lieut. W. I. K. MOON, 2/Lieut. A. G. SPALDING proceeded home on leave.	ate
	3		A & B Coys in the Support trenches THIEPVAL WOOD. C & D Coys found working parties of 145 men daily for various purposes.	ate
	4 to 7		At 11 pm the Enemy opened an intensive from Farmhouse on THIEPVAL WOOD and soon after raided the 1st DORSETS holding the right of G.2. Sector. Our A Coy went to their support and B Coy also sent 2 platoons to support. A Coy being under the command of MAJOR MACRORY. "B" Coy under CAPTAIN ROBERTSON.	ate
	7/8		Our losses were 2 Killed No 15995 Pte SHIELDS. W. and No 23652 Private COLLINS and 6 Wounded, all of 'A' Coy.	ate
	8		The following wire was received from G.O.C. 32nd Division	

WAR DIARY or INTELLIGENCE SUMMARY

Army Form C. 2118.

10th R. INNISKILLING FUSILIERS

Place	Date	Hour	Summary of Events and Information	Remarks and references to Appendices
	May 8.	19.16	"The G.O.C. 32nd Division wishes to thank the 109th Brigade for the very prompt and effective support given to his left Battalion last night. Please convey this warm appreciation of the services they rendered, to all concerned." The Battalion moved to LEALVILLERS going into Divisional Reserve. The following was published by Brig.Gen. HICKMAN commanding 109th Brigade:— "The Brigadier General desires to express to all Officers and men, of the 10th Bn. Royal Inniskilling Fusiliers his appreciation of the behaviour of all ranks whilst in the trenches during the last 3 months. It is a great pleasure to him to feel that the careful training given to all by their Commanding Officers has borne such great fruit. The work they have done and casualties numerous but that there has been shewn, that true sign of Gallant Spirit, determination, and above all good discipline. The Brigadier General hopes that all ranks will enjoy the short period of embarkation not allowed them, and that when they have come, they but return to the firing line to do still more valuable work for their Country." Captain WARING SMYTH reported having returned from Sick Leave Lieut S. DOUGLAS and 2/Lieut E. CRAWLEY proceeded home on leave	etc etc etc etc etc
	9			

WAR DIARY
or
INTELLIGENCE SUMMARY

(Erase heading not required.) 10th Bn. R. Inniskilling Fusiliers

Army Form C. 2118.

Place	Date	Hour	Summary of Events and Information	Remarks and references to Appendices
	May 1916			
V	9		Adjut T. G. SWANN reported having been Segatted to this Battalion.	Apt
Q	11		The Battalion was inspected by the C.in.C (Sir Douglas HAIG.) at CLAIRFAYE. Later on a route march.	Apt
III	12/13/14		The Battalion practised the attack over dummy trenches at CLAIRFAYE FARM. These trenches are an exact copy of the German trenches opposite THIEPVAL WOOD having been laid out from aeroplane photographs.	Apt
Y	14		Major G.H. BRUSH & 2/Lieut & Q. M't. G.G. KENDALL proceeded home on leave.	Apt
Y			Captain F.A. BARTON and 50 other ranks of 'C' Coy proceeded to MARTINSART WOOD as a working party and returned in the evening of the 16th.	Apt
Y	15/16 16/18		On each day the Battalion practised the attack over the Dummy Trenches.	Apt
III	19		Captains. R. S. KNOX and J. C. D PROCTOR proceeded home on leave.	Apt
Y	20/23		The Battn practised the attack over the dummy trenches.	Apt
	24		2/Lieut. W. J SHANNON and 2/Lieut. G. H. PROKMAN proceeded home on leave.	Apt
	25		A draft of 16 men reported on this date	Apt

WAR DIARY
or
INTELLIGENCE SUMMARY 10th Bn. R. Inniskilling Fusiliers

Army Form C. 2118.

Place	Date	Hour	Summary of Events and Information	Remarks and references to Appendices
ATHIES	May 19/16		The Brigade was formed up at CLAIRFAYE at 12 noon and was addressed by Brigadier-General T. HICKMAN who handed over command to Brigadier-General R.G. SHUTER D.S.O. The following is a copy of the farewell order published by Brig. Gen. Hickman. "In bidding good bye to the 109th Brigade, Brig. Gen. Hickman wishes to express to all ranks his most sincere appreciation and thanks for the most loyal support and cordial co-operation which has been given him by everyone in the Brigade since the raising of it in September 1914. Brig. Gen. Hickman cannot adequately express his sorrow at leaving, but duty calls him elsewhere, and duty comes first. Brig. Gen. Hickman with their difficulties and has always watched over their training, & has rejoiced with them Summer in Cannot but be aware of the very high state and rejoiced in their successes the Cannot but be aware of the very high state of efficiency reached by all units. He hopes that the Brigade will always maintain the same "Happy family" as he knows it, that it will continue to draw the good name it has earned and by its future behaviour before the enemy, string get now and add glory to the established Regiments forming it, and which from which it Came."	

Army Form C. 2118.

WAR DIARY
or
INTELLIGENCE SUMMARY
(Erase heading not required.) 10th Bn. R. Innis Killing Fusiliers

Instructions regarding War Diaries and Intelligence Summaries are contained in F. S. Regs., Part II. and the Staff Manual respectively. Title Pages will be prepared in manuscript.

Place	Date	Hour	Summary of Events and Information	Remarks and references to Appendices
LEALVILLE	May 1916 26/27 28 29.		The Battn. practised the attack over the dummy trenches.	ate
			A draft of 13 reported today.	ate
			The following proceeded on leave today. 2/Lieuts. A.N. NESBITT & G.H. GIBSON	ate
	30/31.		The attack again practised	ate

2449 Wt. W14957/Mg0 750,000 1/16 J.B.C. & A. Forms/C.2118/12.

109th Brigade.
36th Division.

1/10th BATTALION

ROYAL INNISKILLING FUSILIERS

JUNE 1916:

Army Form C. 2118.

WAR DIARY
or
INTELLIGENCE SUMMARY

(Erase heading not required.)

10th Bn. R. Inniskilling Fusiliers

Place	Date	Hour	Summary of Events and Information	Remarks and references to Appendices
	June 1916			
	1/2		Ordinary training carried out.	
			The following Divisional (36th Div.) Routine order No 416 was published.	
			Commander-in-Chief's Despatch dated G.H.Q. 19/5/16	
			"Whilst many other units than dared excellent work during the period under review, the following have been specially brought to my notice, in carrying out or repelling trench attacks and raids.	
			x x x x x	
			10th (S) Bn. Royal Inniskilling Fusiliers	
			x x x x x	
			The Divisional Commander congratulates the above unit on having been mentioned in the Commander-in-Chief's Despatch.	
	3		Major F.S.N. MACRORY. Captain J.T.E. MILLER. Captain S.E. PICKEN. R.A.M.C. proceeded home today on leave	
	4/7		The Battalion practiced the attack on all three days.	
	8		Lieut J.N. DRENNAN proceeded on leave	

Army Form C. 2118.

WAR DIARY
or
INTELLIGENCE SUMMARY

(Erase heading not required.)

10th Bn. R Innis Fus

Place	Date	Hour	Summary of Events and Information	Remarks and references to Appendices
	June 1916			
	9/10		Gas attack again. Practised.	
	11		Captain A. F. Cook proceeded to MARTINSART to-day to be attached to the 107th brigade on a course of instruction in Staff Duties. Lieutenant C.N.L. Stronge appointed acting Adjutant during his absence.	
			2/Lt. Swann proceeded on leave to-day.	
	12.		No. SK4 L/Cpl. Hart, London Gazette 2.6.16. No. 15538 Eairick (now Lance-corpl) garrison of "B" company, awarded the Military Medal. The act for which he was recommended was as follows:—	
			"On the night of 20/21 February 1916 he was in charge of a bombing section in the most dangerous post in the REDAN, he about 8 p.m. he was hit in the side by shrapnel, & although at that part of the line the water was knee deep, he refused to leave his post until relieved next morning, when he had become delirious.	
	12		Major J. H. Brush (2nd in command) proceeded to VARRENNES to-day to take over command of the 11th R. Inniskilling Fusiliers, vice Lt/Col. Hessey promoted Brigadier General.	

Army Form C. 2118.

WAR DIARY
or
INTELLIGENCE SUMMARY

(Erase heading not required.)

Instructions regarding War Diaries and Intelligence Summaries are contained in F. S. Regs, Part II. and the Staff Manual respectively. Title Pages will be prepared in manuscript.

Place	Date	Hour	Summary of Events and Information	Remarks and references to Appendices
June	1916			
	14		The Bn moved from LEAVILLERS into bivouacs in AVELUY WOOD. Transport & Q.M. Stores being at FORCEVILLE.	
	15			
	16		On all of these days the Bn was occupied digging trenches in THIEPVAL WOOD.	
	17			
	18			
	19			
	19		2/Lt A.N. Nubik having to be accepted as an observer on Probation in the R.F.C. proceeded to R.F.C. H⁽d⁾ Q⁽rs⁾ to-day.	
	20		2ⁿᵈ Lieut S.E.H.E. Fox 2/Lt J.N. Chisnall, 2/Lt R.S. Fanning & 2/Lt R.J. Neill joined the Bⁿ to-day for the while Battalion on working parties in THIEPVAL WOOD during all	
	21			
	22		these days from 7 a.m. till 6 p.m. each day.	
	23			
	24		The Battalion moved in to MARTINSART WOOD into huts.	
	25		Bombardment of German lines commenced, bombardment on the	
	26		ditto continued, working parties from the Bⁿ were sent up to	
	27		THIEPVAL WOOD on the first three nights of the bombardment.	
	28		Attack postponed Battalion moved back to FORCEVILLE.	
	30		Battalion left FORCEVILLE and proceeded to the trenches strength 20 Officers 742 other Ranks	

list of officers:- Lt. Col Ross Smyth. comdg. Major F.S.N. Macrory 2ⁿᵈ in C. Lieut: C.N.L. Stronge adjutant, Lieut J.E. Austin training officer, 2/Lt E. Gawsley Intelligence officer, 2/Lt J.L. Montgomery signal officer. Capt⁽ⁿ⁾ R.S. Kinnet D coy, Capt⁽ⁿ⁾ J.E. Packer R.A.M.C. medical officer. A Coy:- Capt⁽ⁿ⁾ G. Bustard, Capt⁽ⁿ⁾ J.T. Miller, B Coy:- ... 2/Lt E. McElyn... H. Chillingworth, 2/Lt K. McKenzie, 2/Lt J. Shallsis 2/Lt Shannon, J. Douglas, 2/Lt Reesman F. Strain, Kerr

WAR DIARY
or
INTELLIGENCE SUMMARY

(Erase heading not required.)

Army Form C. 2118.

Place	Date	Hour	Summary of Events and Information	Remarks and references to Appendices
FORCEVILLE	June 27th		C O P Y. S P E C I A L O R D E R O F T H E D A Y. BY MAJOR-GENERAL O.S.W. NUGENT, D.S.O. Commanding 36th. (Ulster) Division. On the eve of the offensive for which the Ulster Division has trained and waited for so many months, I wish that every Officer and man of the Division should know how absolutely confident I feel that the honour of the British Army and the honour of Ulster are in safe keeping in their hands. It has been my privilege to Command the Division in France during the past 9 months, during which time I have had various opportunities of seeing that it has been ever steadfast in defence and gallant in minor offensives. The time has now come to show to the world the qualities which fit it for the great offensive about to open. Much is expected of the Ulster Division and I am certain that the expectation will be fulfilled. Resolution, Self reliance, Discipline and the spirit which knows no surrender and no defeat are present in full measure in every unit of the Division and will bear fruit on the battlefield that will redound to the credit of our country. Nine months ago, the King, after his inspection of the Division desired me to write and tell him how it bore itself, in its first great encounter with the enemy. I know that I shall be able to write and tell how the men of the Ulster Division bore themselves like men in the day of battle and did all that was asked of them. To every Officer and man of the Division I wish succes and honour. (Signed) O.S. Nugent, Major-General, Commanding 36th. Division. 27th. June, 1916.	

109th Brigade
36th Division.

1/10th BATTALION

ROYAL INNISKILLING FUSILIERS

JULY 1916:

WAR DIARY
or
INTELLIGENCE SUMMARY
(Erase heading not required.)

Army Form C. 2118.

Place	Date	Hour	Summary of Events and Information	Remarks and references to Appendices
			REPORT ON OPERATIONS culminating in the Advance on 1.7.16.	

In the first place it must be understood that this account only purports to deal with events concerning this Battalion particularly either directly or indirectly. It will therefore be advisable to summarise shortly the movements and dispositions of the Battalion for a short period immediately preceding the date of the Advance. For some weeks previous to Wednesday 14th June the Battalion had been lying at LEALVILLERS, on which date it moved up to AVELUY WOOD where it bivouaced alongside the rest of the 109th Brigade being employed in the preparation of Assembly Trenches etc., in THIEPVAL WOOD. On Saturday 24th June it moved back to MARTINSART WOOD from whence it was preparing to move up to THIEPVAL WOOD on 28th June when information was received that the Advance had been postponed for two days and that the Battalion was to move back to FORCEVILLE in the interim. As all material for the advance had been issued to the men it was decided to withdraw the heavier stuff and store it at MARTINSART so as to avoid overtiring the men on the seven miles march which they would eventually have to do from FORCEVILLE to the front line trenches. Eventually these stores – bombs – loose burn extra ammunition etc., were dumped near MARTINSART alongside the road by which the battalion advanced to the trenches and were picked up with their ~~parties by the main~~ parties by the main body as it marched through. This arrangement worked well in spite of the darkness and crowded state of the roads but necessitated a great deal of careful preliminary work. On Friday 30th June we received orders to march out of FORCEVILLE at 9.15 p.m. en route for Assembly Trenches which had been carefully reconnoitred and fixed upon beforehand. The start was made punctually by platoons at 100 yards distance going through AVELUY WOOD which was ~~very dark~~ ~~more direct and~~ unknown. The Commanding Officer Lieut-Colonel Ross Smyth had the misfortune to slip and sprain his leg and had to be sent back on an Ambulance. Command was then taken by Major F.S.N. Macrory. Some enemy shelling was experienced from this on but the battalion was fortunate in reaching its Assembly trenches without Casualties. By the time all Coys and details were in position it was after 1 a.m. as the trenches were crowded and progress difficult and slow. Luckily the weather kept fine and the men were in good spirits. Finally arrangements for the assault were now made and the four gaps in our wire (which had been previously cut) were inspected and labelled, look out men being relief posted close to them to direct all troops as to their position. The practical dispositions for the attack may now be provincially summarised. The 10th Bn. Royal Inniskilling Fusiliers occupied a front of approximately 200 yards from the top of INVERNESS AVENUE on the right to the top of ELGIN AVENUE on the left. The ~~object was~~ the objective was the German "C" line from a point C 9 (OMAGH) exclusive – Map Reference R. 20.a.7.4 on the right.

WAR DIARY
or
INTELLIGENCE SUMMARY
(Erase heading not required.)

Army Form C. 2118.

Place	Date	Hour	Summary of Events and Information	Remarks and references to Appendices
			to a point R.20.d.6.6 on the right. This included one strong point known as B.16 (DUNGANNON) which had to be consolidated when captured. As supports, were the 14th Bn. Royal Irish Rifles whose orders were to assist us in holding the "C" line. On our right were the 9th Bn. Royal Inniskilling Fusiliers with the 11th Bn. Royal Inniskilling Fusiliers in similar support. On our left was the 108th Brigade whilst in reserve was the 107th Brigade with orders to pass through us after the "C" line was taken and capture the German "D" line. The battalion dispositions were that "A" Coy., who led the attack on the right supported by "C" Coy., whilst "B" Coy., led the attack on the left supported by "D" Coy. Each Coy., carried picks, shovels and a proportion of R.E. consolidating material and had attached to it a Machine Gun and team from 109th Brigade Machine Gun Coy., whilst strong parties of Bombers and "cleaners up" from the 14th Bn. Royal Irish Rifles. By 6 a.m. there was every probabability of a bright sunny day. An issue of rum was erved round to the men in the trenches. Our bombardment which had been intense all night now became terrific, the enemy retaliating with terrible vigour. At 7 a.m. the Stokes Trench Mortars opened a hurricane bombardment on the enemy front trench with very great effect showers of all earth and debris being thrown high into the air all along this trench. The uproar of the explosion, coming from their sides was now so great that it was difficult to make ones-self heard., but our men preserved their usual cheerful and almost stolid demeanour through everything, grinning happily if one passed— paused to speak to them. A reference to the map will show that our advance had been made at an angle practically half-right to our front line trenches. The famous "sunken road" in "NO MAN'S LAND" just in front of our line is however practically at an direct right angle to the line of advance and it had been carefully impressed on all ranks that to keep the true direction the "sunken road" would be at last as a preliminary forming up place for all our lines. This arrangement was well adhered to by our leading lines but in the excitement of the assault some of the rear "waves" of men advanced straight out of our front trenches and at right angles to that by which error these supporting "waves" reached the german lines much. too far to the left which partly counts for the mixing up of battalions that finally ensued. A more serious error which occured later was that the leading companies twice sufferee heavy loss from our own artillery fire. It is unfair to blame anyone in particular for this regrettable incident as all the senior officers with these companies had fallen at the time and though all ranks knew the time table they quite forgot about it in the impetuous ardour of their ordeal. It is unfortunately not the first time that this accident has happened through the course of the war	

WAR DIARY or INTELLIGENCE SUMMARY

(Erase heading not required.)

Army Form C. 2118.

and its liability is rendered greater by any special gallantry in the troops employed. At 7.15 a.m. on a beautiful summer morning the two leading companies began to issue by platoons through the gaps of our wire into "NO MAN'S LAND" which (were to doubly into extended line which about 3 paces interval and in this formation crept cautiously up toward the leading line was within 100 yards of the german "A" line where it lay down to wait the signal for assault. The three following lines similarly holding and lying down at distances in rear of about 50 yards successfully. Meantime the supporting Coys., "C" and "D" moved forward through THIEPVAL WOOD from their Assembly trenches to the front line trenches just vacated by the leading companies where they prepared to issue in lines of platoons in fours directly the advance was sounded. At 7.30 a.m. sharply the hurricane bombardment of the Stokes Morters ceased and from our front trench came the regimental bugle call followed by the "ADVANCE" Simultaneously Coy and Platoon leaders blew their whistles and the lines of men jumped up and advanced at a steady march past towards the enemy trenches. The spectacle of these lines of men moving forward with rifle sloped and and the morning sun glistening on their fixed bayonets, keeping their alignment and distance as well as if on a Coronation partyrd. Unfaltering unwavering — this spectacle was not only impressive it was extraordinary. Hardly a man was seen to fall in the earlier stage of the advance

108th Brigade had advanced steadily slightly before the time but they had a longer distance to come so that the total alignment was not affected On our right the 9th Inniskillings less fortunate than ourselves suffered as they advanced from enfilade machine gun fire coming from the Thiepval Direction but never failed to preserve their alignment. Every credit is due to our artillery who had done all they had promised us in the matter of getting the enemy's wire-levelling his front trenches. Not a single man of our battalion had occasion as far as one can learn to use his wire cutters of which each Coy., carried a supply.. In the "A" line the leading Coys., were re-inforced by the two supporting Coys., and our barrage having lifted the men sped forward towards the "B" line having killed the few Germans who had so far appeared. The supporting Coy's suffered more in the first part of the advance than the leading ones, the enfilading machine gun fire from Thiepval having evidently increased in intensity. Enemy prisoners now began to come in most of them having evidently been concealed in deep dug-outs in the german support trench which runs close behind their front trench. They seemed for the most part dazed and bewildered by the fury of our bombardment and were only too glad to surrender and throw down their arms. They were sent back under escort to our trenches — about 16 prisoners to each escorting soldier. The first batches of these prisoners were so anxious to reach the shelter of our trenches that they had ototophed their course—screws in the dash recent

WAR DIARY or INTELLIGENCE SUMMARY

Army Form C. 2118.

(Erase heading not required.)

Instructions regarding War Diaries and Intelligence Summaries are contained in F. S. Regs., Part II. and the Staff Manual respectively. Title Pages will be prepared in manuscript.

Place	Date	Hour	Summary of Events and Information	Remarks and references to Appendices
			across the open and meeting our reinforcing lines coming forward were abandoned by them (by attack) in the chest of the moment. Some reached our trenches and were there handed by the few of our men remaining in our front line and were somewhat undeceived as to the true state of affairs. In "B" Line which was captured with apparently little- comparatively little opposition. About 8 a.m. a considerable number of prisoners was taken and the dug-outs were thoroughly bombed whilst waiting for the barage to lift from "C" line. It was here that 2nd Lieut Spalding "B" Coy., was killed by a regrettable mistake. He had decided to bomb a dug-out and was (in advance) when he was shot by a man of one of the rifle regiments who mistook him for a german. A start was next made towards "C" line. The advance was checked for a time owing to the right flank 9th Royal Innis., Fus., being held up by enfilade machine gun fire from Thiepval. And during this check we also suffered a great many casualties from the same cause. On resuming our advance a section of our line/pushed forward to repel and got cut up by our artillery own artillery fire causing further casualties. Directly the barrage lifted from "C" line our men pushed forward and captured the trench. This was about 9 a.m. They found a large number of dead and wounded germans in this line which was at once consolidated by our troops. All available Lewis and Vickers Guns being placed in defensive positions. By this time men from the supporting Battalion (14th Royal Irish Rifles) were pushing to reinforce our men and shortly after the line was further stiffened by the arrival of some of the 107th Brigade. Our right Companies were now largely distributed about the "Crucifix" which they assisted the 9th Royal Innis., Fus., to consolidate. Portions of the left Coys., were apparently at least 200 yards too far to the left of their objective owing to having kept a wrong direction from the start as explained before. In fact by this fact the men of our battalion were more or less intermingled with representatives of all other Brigade of the Ulster Division. It was extremely difficult to locate any position accurately owing to the battered condition of the trenches. Capt Miller ("D" Coy) had already been brought back to our lines severely wounded in the face with shrapnel. Capt Proctor ("C"Coy) was leading his men towards the Crucifix when his leg was shattered by shell fire and he lay in the trench for many hours, but it proved impossible to get him back owing to heavy fire. Eventually Capt Knox who went forward with reinforcements about 5 p.m. carried him back as far as the "A" line where Cap. Proctor died. About noon Capt Robertson "B" Coy., and Lieut Wilton ("A" Coy.) were endeavouring to find their position in "C" line with a map when they were simultaneously struck by rifle fire(locate) the former being wounded in the chin and shoulder and the latter in the chest. Lieut Wilton was assisted back to our lines by one of our N.C.O's-Sergeants PORTER ("B"Coy) was endeavouring to get Capt Robertson back when a bursting shell killed Porter and both fell. No news can since be obtained of Capt Robertson. It will thus be seen that all 2d/Lt Mung 57/2d/Lt ounsoner 2/Lt W.B.Fox woundsd 18/Lt killed during the morning but in spite of this the	

WAR DIARY or INTELLIGENCE SUMMARY

Army Form C. 2118.

(Erase heading not required.)

Place	Date	Hour	Summary of Events and Information	Remarks and references to Appendices
			remaining officers and N.C.O's rallied and organized the men throughout the long and trying day. There could be no doubt that from noon onwards considerable confusion existed and contrary orders were passed from one flank to another. At any time probably about noon some of our men in addition with men of the 107th Brigade attacked and carried the portion of the german "D" line junction which was held for some time till the enemy artillery found the range and inflicted the terrible loss off them. They then fell back to the "C" line and were again assaulted by artillery fire. An order was given by the senior officer on the spot to retire some ten or twenty yards in order to take up a position in a more sheltered trench. The order was taken up promptly and many men who had gallantly held positions rendered almost untenable by artillery and Machine Gun fire for hours undoubtedly got the impression that they were ordered to fall back on Thiepval Wood. A scattered stream of men began to arrive back in our front line, some wounded and all much exhausted by the terrible ordeal they had come through, the time being then about 5 p.m. At this juncture an urgent message was received at Battalion Headquarters from the right flank where Lieut McClure of "C" Coy., was in command of the remnants of our men and was still holding the Crucifix Reinforcements ammunition, bombs called for and perhaps himself the most important of all - water.

The stragglers were hastily rallied and sent forward to the Crucifix under Capt Knox — some 30 men in all. 6 four gallon petrol tins full of water were also sent with a spare party. This party was severely shelled on this journey across "NO MAN'S LAND" and lost several. The survivors were unable to find Lieut McClure's party and handed the water over to men of different Battalions in the "C" line. Capt Knox and his party also failed to find Lieut McClure but great confusion reigned in that district accentuated by terrible shelling and machine gun fire from Thiepval. Many casualties occured and eventually late in the evening a retirement became inevitable. Our front trenches were now being manned from ELGIN AVENUE westward to the river ANCRE by the 16th Royal Iriish Rifles (Pioneers). 5th West Yorkshire Regiment and apparently some coys., of one of the West Riding Regts was the men of the 10th Royal Inniskilling Fusiliers as they returned to our trenches were collected and sent back to their Assembly trenches. A party was sent to Paisley Dump to draw rations and another party to SPEYSIDE for water and the men were made as comfortable as circumstances permitted. At 4 p.m. on 2nd July the order was received to move the battalion back to Martinsart Wood and this was accomplished happily without further loss.

Of 22 officers and 742 other ranks who went into Thiepval Wood on the 30th June 1916 — 10 officers and 336 other ranks returned to Martinsart Wood 2nd July 1916. In addition to | |

Army Form C. 2118.

WAR DIARY
or
INTELLIGENCE SUMMARY
(Erase heading not required.)

Instructions regarding War Diaries and Intelligence Summaries are contained in F.S. Regs., Part II. and the Staff Manual respectively. Title Pages will be prepared in manuscript.

Place	Date	Hour	Summary of Events and Information	Remarks and references to Appendices
	2nd		the officers whose names have been already mentioned as casualties the following were wounded during the course of the fighting and :- Lieuts J. Douglas, McKenzie, and Gibson. The wounded and missing Officers included Lieuts. McClure, Shannon and Kemp. The hope that these officers may be alive still is unfortunately very faint as is also in the case of Capt Robertson.	
	3rd		During the afternoon the Battalion moved out from the front line in Thiepval Wood to the huts in Martinsart Wood which they had left on June 28th. The enemy's artillery continuously shelled the first part of the road but no further casualties occured. The Battalion marched to HEDAUVILLE (5 miles) where they remained in billets for three days.	
	5th		The Battalion to-day marched to HERISSART. (10 miles) where they stayed in billets for four days.	
	10th		The battalion to-day marched to FIENVILLERS via VAL DE MAISON and CANDAS marching thence on the following morning to CONTEVILLE a distance of 8 miles and entrained for	
	11th		BERGUETTE where they arrived at 11.30 p.m. After a halt of half-an-hour during which hot tea was served to the men they again marched another 13 miles to RACQUINGHEM where the	
	12th		battalion arrived at 5.40 a.m. the strength being 22 officers and 415 other ranks. I officer and 50 men having been left at CONTEVILLE for entrainment duties. After an extremely trying journey extending over 13 hours - 21 miles of which was done on foot the men arrived at their billets in excellent condition with no stragglers.	
	13th		The battalion marched with the remainder of the Brigade to a new area and proceeded to billets in ACQUIN via St OMER (16 miles)	
	21st 23rd 27th		The battalion again moved to MERCKINGHEM from whence they proceeded on July 23rd to KORTEPYP by Motor Bus where they remained in huts until the 27th July when they marched 3 miles to PLOEGSTEERT Wood where they were accommodated in Huts.	

War Diary 11th (S) Bn Rl Inniskilling Fusiliers   July 1916.
Appendix 2.   Map showing position of Battalions and Brigades with Objectives during attack

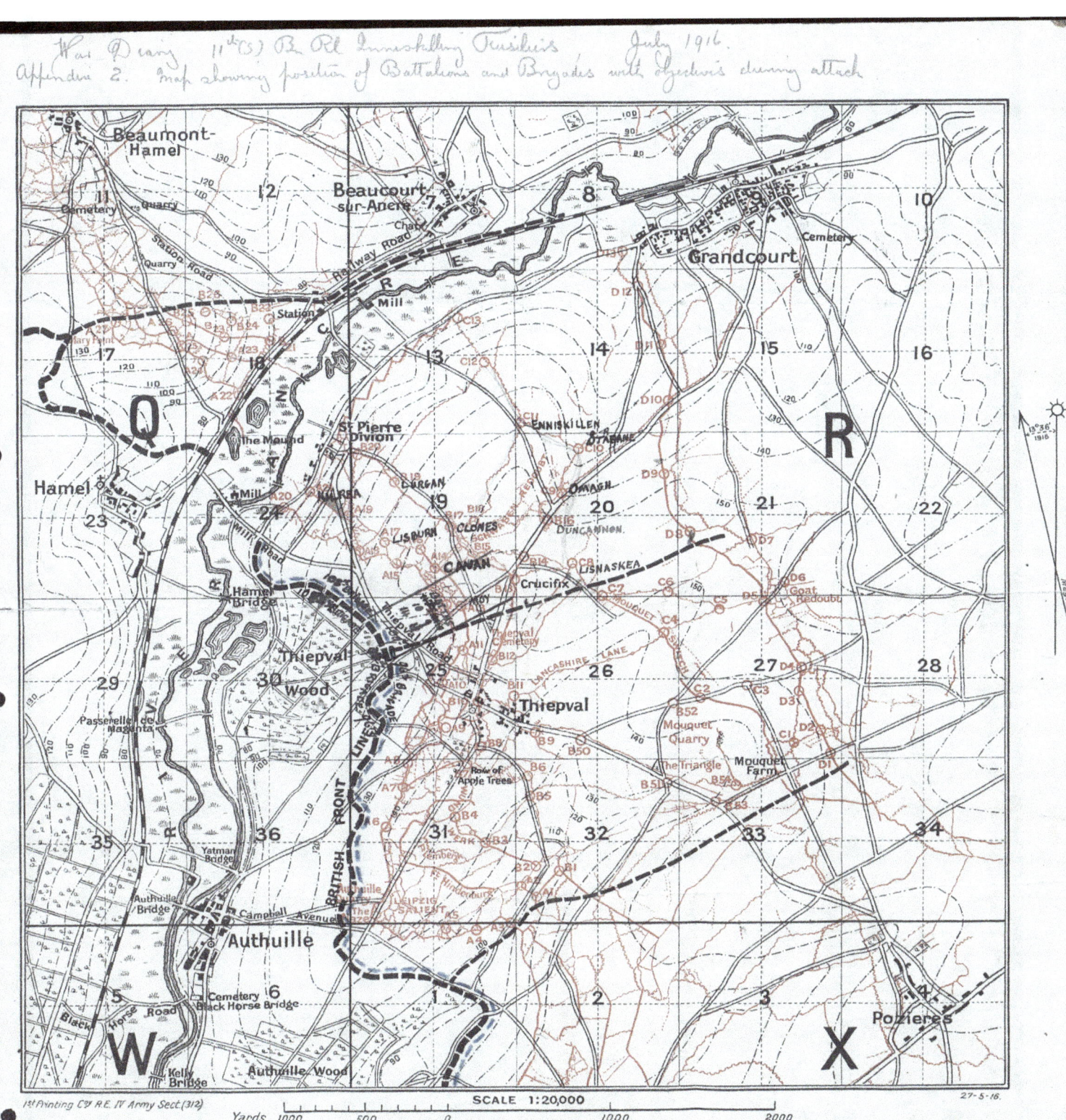

WAR DIARY

of

10TH (S) BATTALION ROYAL INNISKILLING FUSILIERS

FOR MONTH OF AUGUST, 1916.

WAR DIARY or INTELLIGENCE SUMMARY.

CONFIDENTIAL.

Army Form C. 2118.

Place	Date	Hour	Summary of Events and Information	Remarks and references to Appendices
PLOEG-STEERT WOOD	August 2nd		R.Q.M.S. KENNEDY. W. proceed to G.H.Q. Cadet School BLENDECQUES during his absence a/C.Q.M.S. 2/c ARTHUR to company will take over duties of R.Q.M.S.	
"	3rd		The battalion relieved the 14th Royal Irish Rifles in the front line to-day.	Ellwoorey &c. R. Smair Gas.
"			2nd Lt. G.H. PLOWMAN to be O.C. A. company. appointment. 2nd Lt. G.H. PLOWMAN 129 Q Junior two. 2nd Lt. O.C. BEALE having reported for duty is taken on the strength, and posted to B company. Date of commission 1.1.16.	
"	8th		2nd Lt. T.W. MAY. 2nd Lt. G.B. DREA. these officers reported for duty 1st day of 4th Connaught Rangers are taken on strength of Battalion, 2nd Lt. MAY being posted to A coy. & 2nd Lt DREA to D coy.	

WAR DIARY or INTELLIGENCE SUMMARY.

Army Form C. 2118.

Place	Date	Hour	Summary of Events and Information	Remarks and references to Appendices
PLOEGSTEERT WOOD	9th		The Battalion was relieved by the 14th Royal Irish Rifles in the front line, and is now stationed at RED LODGE, PLOEGSTEERT WOOD.	
	15th		Captain & Adjutant F.P. BOYD proceeded to-day to BAILLEUL to instruct the Divisional School of which he is commandant. During his absence Lieut. C.M.L. STRONGE O.C. D company will act as adjutant, 2nd Lt. MOON taking over D. company.	Telegram, St. O.C. "Sheet 35, Jany. 8th"
			2nd Lt. & E.S.S. g. Mc CLENAGHAN. 3rd Bn. R. Irish Fusiliers having reported for duty to-day is taken on the strength of the Battalion, and posted to D company.	
	16th		2nd Lt. E. CRAWLEY is appointed Divisional Drainage Officer, & proceeded to take up his duties to-day.	
	15th		The Battalion relieved the 14th Royal Irish Rifles in the front line to-day.	

WAR DIARY
or
INTELLIGENCE SUMMARY.

(Erase heading not required.)

Army Form C. 2118.

Place	Date	Hour	Summary of Events and Information	Remarks and references to Appendices
DEG STEER T WOOD	16th		Captain F.D. Boyd having been appointed commandant 36th Divisional School the C.N. h. Shope is appointed acting adjutant from 15th inst.	
	21st		14th R. Irish Rifles relieved the Battalion in the front line 15 day.	
	26th 27th		We had a very quiet tour only 1 man being slightly wounded. McCrea joined the unit. During time two nights 420 gas cylinders were carried up in to the front line by the Battalion.	
	28th		Battalion relieved 14th R. Irish Rifles in front line	
	30/31	1.30 a.m.	Gas was released by heavy bombard- ment, by our artillery which was followed from 1.34 - 2.4 a.m. Enemy replied in self-inflicted pattern 14th R. Irish Rifles attempted a raid but were held up by enemy wire, returning without any casualties. During the night we suffered two casualties. 1 killed by trench mortar	
	31st		Regt. S.M. R. J. Kendale left for 10th Bn. South Irish Reg. having been fourth grand [Gayette?] Hr. Trent & [Gentz.] mortar.	

SECRET.   No. 9

F. 238
3rd August 1916.

BATTALION ORDERS
- by -
MAJOR F. S. N. MACRORY,

Commanding 10th (s) Battalion Royal Inniskilling Fus.,

1. **TRENCHES.**

    The Battalion will to-day relieve the 14th Bn. R. Irish Rifles.   Relief will commence at 5 p.m. Details of relief are as follows -
    "A" Coy. to relieve "A" Coy., 14th R. Ir. Rif.
    "C" "   "   "   "B" "   "   "   "   "
    "D" "   "   "   "C" "   "   "   "   "
    "B" "   "   "   "D" "   "   "   "   "

    Order of relief will be as above. Movement to be by Platoons at 200 yards distance.
    Leading Platoon of "A" Coy., to be opposite Headquarters 14th R. Ir. Rif. at 5 p.m.
    Platoons will be met by guides from corresponding platoons of 14th R. Ir. Rif.   Headquarters will close here and open at present Headquarters 14th Bn. R. Ir. Rif. at 5.30 p.m. to-day.

2. **RATIONS.**

    Quartermaster will send 4 Dixies for each of following Companies, "A", "B", and "D" to go with rations this evening.
    Cooker of "B" Coy., to take place of the cooker of "D" Coy., 14th Bn. R. Ir. Rif on road.
    Cooking of "A" "C" and "D" Coys., will be done in Trenches by means of Dixies - Charcoal and Coke has been indented for.   Cooking of "B" Coy and Headquarters will be done on Cooker of "B" Coy.,

3. **TRENCH STORES.**

    Copies of List of Trench Stores taken over are to be at ORDERLY ROOM not later than 12 hours after taking over.

4. **REPORT**

    Coys., will immediately on their reliefs being complete in every detail send a written certificate to this effect by runner to Battalion Headquarters.

5. **FORT OXFORD.**   The section at Fort Oxford will be relieved by 14th Bn. R. Ir. Rif. before 5 p.m. to-day.

6. **COMMUNICATIONS.**

    One runner per Coy., to report for duty at Battalion Headquarters at 5 p.m. to-day.
    Coy Commanders will ensure that selected Coy., runners know as soon as relief is completed, the positions of Battalion Headquarters and Headquarters of other Coys.,
    Headquarters and Coy Signallers will report at Headquarters 14th Bn. R. Ir. Rif. at 2 p.m. to-day to take over duties in advance.

7. **LEWIS GUNS.**

    Lewis Gun Teams and the Lewis Gun Officer report at Headquarters 14th Bn. R. Ir. Rif. at 2 p.m. to-day to take over duties in advance.

No._____ ACQUITTANCE ROLL (ALL ARMS) Army-Form N 1513.

{ Squadron / Battery / Company } of the _____

Imprest a/c No. _____

Regl. No.	RANK AND NAME.	*Adapt if necessary.	Cash Payment.		Sterling Equivalent (To be completed in Fixed-centre Pay Office).		Receipt of Soldier.
			Francs	Centimes	s.	d.	

Total

To be inserted by Paying Officer. Total, in words—

Francs_____

Centimes_____

The undermentioned (1) and (2) to be completed by Paymaster i/c Clearing House—
(1) Rate of Exchange—5 _____ = _____ s. d.
(2) Total Sterling equivalent, in words—

_____ Pounds, _____ Shgs., and _____ Pence.

Signature of the Officer making the Payments _____

Date of Payment _____ 19 .   Officer Commanding _____ Coy.,

_____ Regt.

Certified that the above amounts have been charged in the ledger accounts of the men concerned.

Date _____ 19 .   _____ Paymaster

(2)

8. BOMBS. L/Corpl. McIntyre will take over Bomb supplies and will act as in para 7 of these.

9. SECRECY.

Immediately on completion of reliefs these orders are to be destroyed by the Battalion Officers to whom they are issued.

(Signed) F. D. BOYD,

Capt & Adjutant.

```
No. 1  - 109th Brigade.
    2  - O.C. "A" Coy.,
    3  - O.C. "B"  "
    4  - O.C. "C"  "
    5  - O.C. "D"  "
    6  - Lewis Gun Officer
    7  - Quartermaster
    8  - Second-in-Command
    9  - O.C. 14th Bn. R. Ir. Rifles
   10  - FILE.
```

Army Form N 1513.

ACQUITTANCE ROLL (ALL ARMS).

No. _____

Squadron
Battery } of the _____
Company

Imprest a/c No. _____

Regtl No.	RANK AND NAME. (Adapt if necessary)	Francs	Centimes	Sterling Equivalent (To be completed in Fixed-centre Pay Office) s. d.	Cash Payment	Receipt of Soldier

The O.C., 14th R.I. Rifles

The undermentioned (1) and (2) to be completed by Paymaster a/c Clearing House—

Total

(1) Rate of Exchange—5 = ─/4
(2) Total Sterling equivalent, in words—

Francs _____ Centimes _____
Pounds _____ Shgs. _____ and Pence _____

To be inserted by Paying Officer. Total, in words—

Signature of the Officer making the Payments _____

Date of Payment _____ 19 .   Officer Commanding _____ Coy.
                                                                Regt.

Certified that the above amounts have been charged in the ledger accounts of the men concerned.

Date _____ 19 .   Paymaster

Secret

No. 2

F. 253.
14.8.16.

BATTALION ORDERS
– by –
MAJOR F. S. N. MACRORY,
Commanding 10th Battalion Royal Inniskilling Fusiliers.

1. TRENCHES. The Battalion will relieve "D" Battalion to-morrow in right sub-sector of the trenches.

2. RELIEFS. (INTELLIGENCE SCOUTS
(SIGNALLERS
(LEWIS GUN TEAMS
(HEADQUARTERS BOMBERS   WILL RELIEVE AS ABOVE at 2.00 p.m. to-morrow. Headquarters will relieve at 5.00 p.m. to-morrow.

Coys., will move to relief by Platoons at 200 yards distance in following order and will take over from the Coys., of "D" Battalion as shown opposite –

COY.,	TRENCH SECTOR	COY OF "D" Battalion.
C	Left	B
A	Centre	A
B	Right	D
D	Subsidiary Line	C

Leading Platoon of "C" Coy., will move from here at 5 p.m. The Battalion Orderly Officer will remain behind to collect certificates re all quarters being handed over.

3. GUARDS. All present Guards will be relieved by D Battalion at 4 p.m. to-morrow.
Guards of D Battalion behind Trenches will be relieved at 5 p.m. by Guards furnished by Police and Coy in Subsidiary Line (D Coy.,)

4. COOKING. A, B, and C Coys., will take Dixies into trenches with them. Cooker of "D" Coy., will go into place on road near Battalion Headquarters.

5. BAGGAGE. All spare kit and stores not required in trenches to be at side of road at C and D Coys., Lines at 4 p.m. to-morrow. Officers servants will load this on to waggons. Quartermaster will detail the Transport to convey above baggage to Quartermaster's Store.

6. REPORTS. Completion of relief to be notified by Coys., in CODE to Battalion Headquarters.

7. HEADQUARTERS. This office will close here and open at Trench Headquarters at 5.30 p.m. to-morrow.

(Signed)
F. D. BOYD,
Capt & Adjutant.

Copies to –
No 1 Headquarters 109th Brigade.
2. "D" Battalion
3. O. Commanding
4. O.C. "A" Coy.,
5. O.C. "B" "
6. O.C. "C" "
7. O.C. "D" "
8. Lewis Gun Officer
9. Signalling Officer
10. Quartermaster
11. Regimental Sergt Major.
12. FILE.

No. 2.

F. 260

RELIEF ORDERS
– by –
Lieut-Colonel F. S. N. MACRORY,
Commanding 10th (s) Battn. Royal Inniskilling Fus.

1. The 14th Bn. R. Ir. Rif. will relieve the 10th Bn. R. Innis., Fusiliers by day in the right sub sector, relief not to commence before 5 p.m. to)morrow 21st inst.,

   Lewis Gun, Intelligence Scouts and Signallers will relieve during the afternoon.

2. Transport lines will not be moved.

3. LOG BOOKS and Diaries of work in hand will be completed and handed over to relieving Battalion.

4. Completion of relief will be reported to Battalion Headquarters in CODE.

5. Company for duty will take over Guards during afternoon, at RED LODGE.

6. Companies to send 1 Officer and 1 N.C.O. to take over billets from 14th Bn. R. Ir. Rif.,

7. Before leaving trenches Company Commanders will get a certificate signed by relieving company stating that trenches have been left in a clean condition.

8. Officers Kit and Mess Boxes to be on road opposite Battalion Headquarters at 4 p.m. – Quartermaster will send Transport to take it to RED LODGE.

(sgd) C. N. L. STRONGE,
Captn. & a/Adjnt.

1. 109th Brigade.
2. 14th Bn. R. Ir. Rif.
3. Commanding Officer
4. Adjutant
5. O.C. "A" Coy.,
6. O.C. "B" "
7. O.C. "C" "
8. O.C. "D" "
9. Lewis Gun Officer
10. Signalling Officer
11. Transport Officer
12. Quartermaster
13. Regt. Sgt Major
14. FILE
15. CANTEEN.
16. Intelligence Officer.

SECRET.
No. 2
F. 869.
27.8.16.

RELIEF ORDERS
- by -
Lieut-Colonel F. S. N. MACRORY,
Commanding 10th (s) Battalion Royal Inniskilling Fusiliers.

1. TRENCHES.
The 10th Royal Inniskilling Fusiliers will relieve 14th Bn. Royal Irish Rifles in right sub-sector to-morrow 28th inst.

2. RELIEFS.
Intelligence Scouts, Headquarters Bombers, Signallers and Lewis Gun Teams will relieve at 3 p.m.
Headquarters will relieve at 5 p.m.
Companies will move to relief by Platoons at 200 yards distance in following order and will take over from Coys., of 14th Bn. Royal Irish Rifles as shewn below-

"A" Company from LEFT COY., 14th Bn. Royal Irish Rifles.
"B"   "   " CENTRE COY.,   "   "   "
"D"   "   " RIGHT COY.,   "   "   "
"C"   "   SUBSIDIARY LINE.

Leading Platoon of "A" Coy., will move from RED LODGE at 5 p.m. The Battalion Orderly Officer will collect all Certificates re all quarters being handed over clean.

3. GUARDS.
All present Guards will be relieved by 14th Bn. Royal Ir. Rif. at 4 p.m. Guards of 14th Bn. Royal Ir. Rif. will be relieved at 4 p.m. by guards furnished by Police and Coy., in Subsidiary Line (C Coy.,)

4. COOKING.
"A", "B", "D" Coys., will take Dixies into trenches with them. Cooker of "C" Coy., will go into shelter on road opposite Battalion Headquarters.

5. STORES.
All spare kit and stores not required in trenches to be at UNDERHILL FARM at 4 p.m. Officers servants will load this into waggons sent up by Transport Officer.
All kit and stores going to the trenches to be at RED LODGE at 4.30 p.m. Officers servants will load this on waggons and accompany it up.

6. REPORTS.
Completion of relief to be notified by Coys., in CODE to Battalion Headquarters.

7. HEADQUARTERS.
This office will close here at 4 p.m. and re-open at Trench Headquarters at 5.30 p.m.

(sgd) C.N.L. STRONGE,
Capt & A/Adjutant.
10th Bn. Royal Inniskilling Fusiliers.

Copies to:-
1. 109th Brigade.
2. "D" Battalion.
3. Commanding Officer
4. O.C. "A" Coy.,
5. O.C. "B" Coy.,
6. O.C. "C" Coy.,
7. O.C. "D" Coy.,
8. Lewis Gun Officer
9. Signal Officer
10. Quartermaster
11. Transport Officer
12. Bombing Officer
13. Intelligence Officer
14. R.S.M.
15. FILE
16. 2nd-in-Command.

Vol 10

Confidential

L.B. 10.0
6 sheets

War Diary

of

10th Bn. Royal Inniskilling Fusiliers.

From 1st September 1916
To 30th September 1916.

[Stamp: 10th Service Battalion, Royal Inniskilling Fusiliers, No. 1848, Date 1/16]

The D.A.G.,
3rd. Echelon.
Base.

per. Headquarters,
109th. Brigade.

Army Form C. 2118.

10th Bn Royal Inniskilling Fusiliers

I

WAR DIARY
or
INTELLIGENCE SUMMARY.
(Erase heading not required.)

Instructions regarding War Diaries and Intelligence Summaries are contained in F. S. Regs., Part II. and the Staff Manual respectively. Title pages will be prepared in manuscript.

Place	Date	Hour	Summary of Events and Information	Remarks and references to Appendices
Plagsteert	Sept 1st	1.30 A.M.	Gas was released by us and followed by artillery bombardment. Enemy artillery replied. We suffered 6 casualties, 1 gunner, 3 gunners were attached to Trench Mortar Battery, one of whom was killed. Our attack appeared to be successful.	
	Sept 3rd 5 pm		The 14th R. Irish Rifles relieved us today in the right subsector.	
	Sept 2nd	11-3.30 pm	There was a false gas-alarm and artillery bombardment for a short time. We had two patrols out at the time but suffered no casualties.	
	Sept 4	1.45 p.m.	The Bn. moved to DRANOUTRE via NEUVE EGLISE relieving the 8th GLOUCESTERS and being relieved by 10th WORCESTERS. The 10th WORCESTERS had 9 killed and about 15 wounded by shell fire about 1 mile in the DRANOUTRE side of NEUVE EGLISE, our Bn. had no casualties although some shells fell within a short distance of them. 2 LIEUT. T. G. SWAN returned to the Bn. from hospital. 2 LIEUT. J. N. CHINNECK went to hospital today about 12 noon.	
	Sept 5th		In the afternoon a few shells were dropped on the far side of DRANOUTRE doing no damage. N.36.a.	
	Sept 6th	6.30 p.m.	The Bn. relieved the 8th N. STAFFORDS in the line.(ref. map sheet 28 1/10000) 2 LIEUT. J. M. MONTGOMERY was slightly wounded in the hand by shrapnel at R.E. FARM. and the 8th N. STAFFORDS suffered 6 casualties at the same time.	

WAR DIARY
or
INTELLIGENCE SUMMARY.

(Erase heading not required.)

Army Form C. 2118.

Place	Date	Hour	Summary of Events and Information	Remarks and references to Appendices
	Sept/	12ᵗʰ	The Bn. were relieved in the line by the 14ᵗʰ R. Irish Rifles, and then moved in to Brigade reserve at AIRCRAFT FARM. During the tour enemy MINNENWERFER were fairly active and lots of our trenches were badly knocked in. We had 19 casualties altogether (8 killed). Our snipers got one certain kill. Our T. Mortars did some excellent work in retaliation. There was one false gas alarm during this tour, apparently it started in the German trenches.	
	12ᵗʰ–18ᵗʰ		Being in Brigade reserve the Bn. had to supply day and night working parties to the trenches, our artillery during this time was very active, hf the German retaliation was practically nil.	
	18ᵗʰ		Relieved the 14ᵗʰ R. Irish Rifles in the line. Trenches very wet, & several trays of right coy. in line are concealed up by Trench Mortars.	
	Sept/21ˢᵗ	3 p.m.	Our Trench Mortars bombarded the German lines for 1 hr. Enemy retaliation weak. Enemy Trenches badly damaged.	
	22ⁿᵈ	6 A.M.	Enemy Trench mortars opened fire, Jerry's retaliated doing little damage.	
	24ᵗʰ		The 14ᵗʰ R.I.R. relieved the Bn. Today and we proceeded to WAKEFIELD HUTS where we were in Divisional Reserve.	
	25ᵗʰ		2 Lt. N.C. Griffith taken on the strength of the Bn.	

WAR DIARY
or
INTELLIGENCE SUMMARY.

(Erase heading not required.)

Army Form C. 2118.

III

Place	Date	Hour	Summary of Events and Information	Remarks and references to Appendices
	Sept. 27th		A German Aeroplane fellow ours brought down near Kemmel Hill. The Sole occupant, an officer, was taken prisoner by two of our men who found part of our raiding party, crashed near the spot. 2/Lt. T.W. Hay and Lieut. H.F. Chillingworth being evacuated to England have been struck off the strength. 2/Lt. G.H. Plowman, Transfer on probation to R.F.C., is struck off the strength.	
	28th		Lt. Battalion were given an outing in Bailleul being entertained by the "Merry Mauves" and then to tea at the 110th Field Amb. the Bn. relieved the 14R Irish Rifles in the line.	
	30th	10.1p.m.	A Raiding Party under command of Lieut. G.H. Webb with 2 Lieuts. T. McCrea and 14 St. G. McClenaghan left our trenches at 10.1 p.m. At about 10.36 p.m. they succeeded in blowing up the Bosch wire and affected an entrance into their front line. According to prearranged signal, our artillery opened fire on the enemy 2nd line, avoided that flanking fire by both machine guns and Stokes Mortars. The Party met with no resistance in the front line, it having	

WAR DIARY
or
INTELLIGENCE SUMMARY.

Army Form C. 2118.

IV

(Erase heading not required.)

Place	Date	Hour	Summary of Events and Information	Remarks and references to Appendices
			apparently been evacuated in a great hurry as the bags were left with rifles & bayonets still on the fire-step. The party remained in the trenches for ½ hour when they were recalled by a bugle sounding the fire-alarm. Amongst the loot brought back was, 1 Machine gun, about 15 Rifles, S.A.A. Ammunition, 1 full kit, 2 cups, a large number of Stick grenades, and some pits bags containing ex ordements. Only one Boch was seen, but they were unable to catch him and any dugouts encountered were empty. The party consisted of about 75 O.R. with 8 R.E's. Our casualties were 14 wounded and 1 R.E. Cpl. killed.	Signed [illegible] O.C. "B" [illegible]

BATTALION ORDERS   F.271.
- by -   3.9.16.
Lieut-Colonel F.S.N. Macrory,
Commanding 10th. Battalion Royal Inniskilling Fuslrs.

1. The 14th. Bn. Royal Irish Rifles will relieve the 10th. Bn. Royal Innis. Fus. this afternoon in the right sub Sector. Relief not to commence before 5 p.m. Lewis Gunners, Signallers, Intelligence Scouts and Battn. Bombers will relieve at 3.30 p.m.

2. Log Books and Diaries of work in hand will be completed and handed over to relieving Unit.

3. Before leaving trenches Company Commanders will get a Certificate signed by relieving Company stating that trenches have been left in a clean and sanitary condition.

4. Officers kit and Mess Boxes to be on Road opposite Battn. Headquarters at 4 p.m. Transport officer will arrange to have wagons there to take it to RED LODGE

5. Companies will send 1 Officer and 1 N.C.O. to take over billets from the 14th. Royal Irish Rifles during the afternoon.

6. Company for duty ("B" Coy.) will take over Guards at RED LODGE before 4 p.m.
1 Cpl., 3 L/C 11 and 12 men to report to the R.S.M. from "B" Coy. at Battalion Headquarters at 3 p.m. for the above Guards.

7. Completion of Relief will be sent to Battalion Headquarters in code.

8. Transport lines will not be moved.

(Signed) C.H.L. Strong,
C ... /Adjt.

Operation File

F. 280.
11.9.16.

SECRET.

RELIEF ORDERS
by
Lieut-Colonel F. S. N. MACRORY,
Commanding 10th Battalion Royal Inniskilling Fusiliers

1. RELIEF. 14th Battalion Royal Irish Rifles will relieve the Battalion in the right sub sector to-morrow (12th inst.,) afternoon. Relief not to commence before 6 p.m.
Lewis Gunners, signallers, Battalion Scouts and Bombers will relieve during the afternoon. Intelligence Officer will have a guide at DAYLIGHT CORNER at 3 p.m. to meet above details.

2. GUIDES. 1 Guide per platoon will report to R.S.M. at Bn. H.Q. at 5.15 p.m., he will send them to DAYLIGHT CORNER to be there by 6 p.m. to meet platoons of 14th R. Ir. Rif.

3. LOG BOOKS. Owing to their being no Log Books Coys., will make out a Diary of work on ordinary paper and hand over to relieving unit.

4. CERTIFICATES. before leaving trenches Coys will get certificate signed by relieving Coy., stating that trenches have be been left in a clean and sanitary condition.

5. ORDER OF RELIEF.

14th R. Ir Rif.		10th R. Innis., Fus.
"A"	will relieve	"C"
"B"	"	"D"
"D"	"	"B"
"C"	"	"A"

6. KIT. Officers Kit and Mess Boxes to be at R.E. FARM by 8.30 p.m. these will be brought back by Transport of 14th R. Ir. Rif, servants will remain with the Kit. Headquarters Kit to be at Cooker Farm at same time.

7. REST BILLETS. "A" Coy., will take over from Coy., of 11th Royal Innis., Fus., at DAYLIGHT CORNER - B, C and D Coys and Headquarters will take over from remaining Coys., of 11th R. Inniskillings at AIRCRAFT FARM.

8. MOVEMENTS. All movements will be by Platoons at 5 mins. interval. Any movement in the open will be by parties of not more than 10 in number at 5 mins. interval.

9. Completion of relief will be reported to Battalion Headquarters in code.

10. TRANSPORT. Transport Lines will not be moved.

(sgd) C.N.L. STRONGE,
Capt & Adjutant,

SECRET.

RELIEF ORDERS.

No. 286.
17.9.16.

by

Lieut-Colonel F.S.N. Macrory,
Commanding 10th. Battalion Royal Inniskilling Fus.

1. The Battalion will relieve the 14th. Royal Irish Rifles in the Right Sub Sector to-morrow.

2. Lewis Gunners, Signallers, and Headquarters Bombers will relieve during the afternoon, and will not leave AIRCRAFT FARM before 2 p.m. 2/Lieut. Montgomery will be in charge of the Signallers and 2/Lieut. Davidson in charge of Lewis Gunners, 2nd./Lieut. Cronin in charge of Bombers.

3. Relief will be via KINGSWAY.

4. Companies will take over as follows:-

10th. Inniskillings.	14th. Rifles.
"A" Company from	Right Company (in line)
"B" " "	Left " (in line)
"C" " "	Mineshafts.
"D" " "	R. E. FARM.

   Companies will move in above order, first platoon of "A" Coy. to be at DAYLIGHT CORNER at 6 p.m. All movements will be by platoons at 5 minutes interval, any movements in the open will be by parties of not more than 10 in number, at 5 minutes interval.

5. Companies will take over the same tactical dispositions as are in force in the Companies they relief.

6. Companies will take over Log Books, Trench Stores and Programme of Work in hand, and will forward a list of the Trench Stores to reach this office by 11 a.m. sharp on the morning after being relieved.

7. Officers Trench Kit and Mess Kit to be at AIRCRAFT FARM at 8 p.m. ready to be put on Transport for trenches, officers servants will remain with kit.

8. Officers valises and spare kit to be at AIRCRAFT FARM at 2 p.m. to go back to TRANSPORT lines, officers servants will load this on wagons.

9. Rations will be at R.E. Farm at 9 p.m. Rations and Kit going to Cooker Farm will be taken up by Pack Mules.

10. Each Company will send 1 Officer and 1 N.C.O. up at 2 p.m. to take over trenches. A certificate will be obtained from incoming Coys. of 14th. R.I. Rifles as to billets handed over being clean and sanitary.

11. Transport Lines will not be moved.

12. Guides of the 14th. Rifles will meet platoons at COOKER FARM on their way up.

13. Completion of relief will be wired in code to Battalion Headquarters.

(Signed) C.N.L. Stronge,
Captain & Adjutant.

CONFIDENTIAL

WAR DIARY

of

10TH BATTALION ROYAL INNISKILLING FUSILIERS

for period from

1ST OCTOBER, 1916.
to
31ST OCTOBER, 1916.

Army Form C. 2118.

WAR DIARY
or
INTELLIGENCE SUMMARY.
(Erase heading not required.)

Place	Date	Hour	Summary of Events and Information	Remarks and references to Appendices
	Oct 1st 1916	2 P.M.	Our Trench mortars were active for a short time but enemy did not reply.	
	Oct 2nd	3 pm	Trench mortars active as usual.	
			This morning the Boche started a strafe. Much damage was done except where trenches were blown in, at two places, men in front line.	
	Oct 3rd		The Boche started the strafe again this afternoon. He blew up our form two Gun trench, killing one man, wounding another. 2 F.A. men Montgomery got shell shock and was sent down to hospital.	
	Oct 4th	7-15pm	The Boche gave us quite a fierce bombardment for 1 hour with trench mortars, shrapnel & H.E. 2 F.A. Beds and one man were killed in the support line. Our trenches were completely blocked in some places, no communication direct being possible between the two front coys. We returned the Boche with trench mortars & artillery for one hour. His reply was weak.	
	Oct 5th			
	Oct 6th	2 A.M.	We used to have put over gas but the wind changed and it commenced to rain, so others were cancelled. The 14th R.I.R. relieved us today in the right sub sector. We went back to DERRY HUTS as Brigade Reserve. Let off the gas successfully in the line. The Div. Band performed	
	Oct 8th			

1577 Wt. W10791/1773 500,000 1/15 D. D. & L. A.D.S.S./Forms/C. 2118.

WAR DIARY
or
INTELLIGENCE SUMMARY.

(Erase heading not required.)

Army Form C. 2118.

Place	Date	Hour	Summary of Events and Information	Remarks and references to Appendices
	1916			
	Oct 10		behind our huts today in the afternoon. We received notification that Capt. J.R. Wilton and R.S.M. White have been awarded the Military Cross.	
	Oct 12		We relieved the 14th R.I.R. in the Regt. Subsector. This afternoon	
	Oct 13		the Boche were reported when attempted a raid on our Regt. front company but were driven off with bomb & Lewis gun fire	
	Oct 14		2 Lt A.S. Lees was wounded this evening when out wiring.	
	Oct 16		We received notification today that the Lewis gun, captured on the wing LL of the raid, has been presented by the Regt. to be placed for exhibition in the quarter Ironmongery.	
	Oct 18		The 14 R.I.R relieved us today in the Regt Subsector and we came back into Div. Reserve at Wakefield Hts.	
	Oct 20		Pte held 2dth first day of our Regt. Sports, the Div. band attended.	
	Oct 21		The finals from sports have been run off today, also its final inter-Coy football match. "A" Coy beating "B" Coy by 2 goals to 1.	
	Oct 22 3 p.m.		A lecture on "Picking up of Message on telephone" by Sunday was given to all Officers & senior N.C.O.'s by Captain Vignoux, Divisional Signal Coy. afterwards very instructive.	
	Oct 24		The Battalion went back into trenches today, relieving the 14th R.I.R. Matters wrote today. Much rain fell.	
	Oct 25		The enemy Trench mortars on trenches about 3 p.m. for an hour. Very little damage done to the line, but 2/Cpl. Wootton was killed by a trench mortar & Pte. McAleer severely wounded.	

Army Form C. 2118.

WAR DIARY
or
INTELLIGENCE SUMMARY.
(Erase heading not required.)

Instructions regarding War Diaries and Intelligence Summaries are contained in F. S. Regs., Part II. and the Staff Manual respectively. Title pages will be prepared in manuscript.

Place	Date	Hour	Summary of Events and Information	Remarks and references to Appendices
	26 Oct.		The weather improved somewhat on this day, but the wire collapsed again the following day.	
	28 Oct.		Head Quarter Dug. Out at COOKER FARM nearly collapsed due to the wet, but was eventually repaired by am Pioneers on 29th.	
	29 Oct.		Lieut. Smartt (assistant adjutant) left on leave this evening.	
	30 Oct.		Battalion was relieved in the line by 1/4th R. I. R. & marched to LOCK & DERRY LODGE & FARM where it billeted.	
	31 Oct.		All men re. went to Divisional Baths at ATRANOUTRE for baths & change of clothing. A Battalion Kit Inspection was held afterwards by C.O. and the usual trench warfare re-commenced in the evening.	

H.U. Mackay, Lt. Colonel.
O.C. 10th R. Irish Rif.

SECRET.   F. 304.
                                                5.10.16.
                    RELIEF ORDERS
                         - by -
                    Major R. S. KNOX,
            Commanding 10th Bn. Royal Inniskilling Fusiliers.

1.   The Battalion will be relieved by the 14th Bn. R. Ir.
        Rif. to-morrow.
            Relief not to commence before 5 p.m. Battalion
        will withdraw into Brigade Reserve at AIRCRAFT FARM
        relieving the 11th Bn. Royal Inniskilling Fusiliers.

2.   Lewis Gunners, Signallers, Battn., Bombers and
        Intelligence Scouts will relieve at 3 p.m.

3.   Route will be via KINGSWAY TRENCH.

4.   All movements will be by platoons at 5 minutes
        interval.
            No movement to take place over the open.

5.   Coys., will take over same tactical dispositions
        as are in force in the Coys., they relieve.

6.   Coys., will hand over lists of Trench Stores, Log
        Books and programmes of work to incoming Coys., of
        14th Bn. Royal Ir. Rif.

7.   2nd Lieut DAVIDSON will take over for all Coys., and
        Bn. Headquarters during the afternoon - 1 N.C.O.
        per Coy., will also be sent to guide Coys. to their
        quarters.

8.   Coy., Officers Kits and Mess Kit to be at R.E. FARM
        at 5.30 p.m.   Headquarters Kit to be ready at
        7.30 p.m. at COOKER FARM. Officers servants will
        remain with Kit, which will be brought back by
        Transport of 14th Bn. Royal Ir. Rif.

9.   Lists of Trench Stores taken over at AIRCRAFT FARM
        to be rendered to this office by 11a.m. 7th inst.,

10.   Transport Lines will not be moved.

11.   Completion of relief to be reported to Bn. Headquarters
        in CODE.

                            (sgd) C.N.L. STRONGE,
                                  Captain & Adjutant.

Issued at 10 p.m. 5.10.16.

    Copies to :-
1. 109th Brigade.   7. O.C. "D" Coy.,
2. 14th Bn. Royal Ir. Rif.   8. Quartermaster.
3. 11th Bn. Royal Innis. Fus., 9. Transport Officer
4. O.C. "A" Coy.,   10. Lewis Gun Officer
5. O.C. "B" Coy.,   11. Commanding Officer
6. O.C. "C" Coy.,   12. FILE.

SECRET.

RELIEF ORDERS   F.310.
by
         11.10.16.

Major R.S. Knox,
Commanding 10th. Bn. Royal Inniskilling Fusrs.

1. The Battalion will relieve the 14th. Royal Irish Rifles in the line to-morrow, 12th. October, 1916. Relief not to begin before 4.30 p.m.

2. Lewis Gunners, Signallers, and Battalion Bombers will relieve at 3 p.m. They must be marched as formed parties under an Officer or senior N.C.O.

3. Route will be via KINGSWAY.

4. All movement will be by platoons at 5 minutes interval. No movement to take place over the open.

5. Men marching to the trenches must be marched correctly as a formed party under an officer, N.C.O. or senior soldier.

6. Companies to take over same tactical dispositions as are in force in the Companies they relieve.

7. All trench stores, log books, and programmes of work will be taken over.
List of Stores to reach Orderly Room by 11 a.m. on morning of 12th. inst.

8. Order of Relief:-
"A" Company to Right front line.
"B"   "   " Left   "   "
"C"   "   " R.E. Farm.
"D"   "   " Battle Headquarters & S. Mine Shaft.

9. All spare kit to be ready at 2.30 p.m. Transport Officer will arrange to take this back to Stores. Trench Kit to be ready at 5.30 p.m. at AIRCRAFT FARM officers servants will accompany this kit to trenches.

10. Transport Lines will not be moved.

11. Battalion Orderly Officer will collect certificates for Billets and hand in to Orderly Room.

12. Completion of Relief to be reported in Code to Battalion Headquarters.

(Signed)   C.N.L. Stronge,
                 Captain & Adjutant.

14th BATTALION,
ROYAL IRISH RIFLES.
RN 1276
11.10.16

F. 395.
28.10.16.

RELIEF ORDERS
- by -
Lieut-Colonel F. S. N. MACRORY,
Commanding 10th Battalion Royal Inniskilling Fusiliers.

1. The Battalion in Right sub-sector will be relieved to-morrow by the 14th Bn. Royal Irish Rifles. Relief not to commence before 2.30 p.m.
    The Battalion on relief will move into Brigade Reserve at DERRY HUTS relieving the 11th Bn. Royal Innis Fus.,

2. Lewis Gunners, Signallers, Battalion Bombers and Scouts will relieve at 12.30 p.m. They must be marched as formed parties under an Officer, N.C.O. or senior soldier.

3. Route will be via KINGSWAY TRENCH.

4. All movements will be by platoons at 5 minutes interval. No movements will take place over the open.

5. Men marching to or from the trenches must be marched as a formed party under an Officer, N.C.O. or senior soldier.

6. Lewis Gun handcarts must not be used for carrying men's packs etc.,

7. All units will take over the same tactical dispositions which were in force in the battalion they relieve.

8. All Coys.; will hand over Trench Stores, Log Books and Programmes of Work to the relieving Unit.

9. Coy., Officers Kit and Mess Kit to be at R.E. FARM at 4 p.m. Headquarters Kit to be ready to COOKER FARM at 5.30 p.m.
    Officers servants will remain with these kits which will be brought back by the Transport of the 14th Bn. Royal Irish Rifles.

10. Lists of Stores taken over at DERRY HUTS to reach this office by 10 a.m. the day after relief.

11. Transport Lines will not be moved.

12. 2/Lieut. Richards will take over for all Coys., and H.Q. during the afternoon. 1 N.C.O. will also be sent from each Coy., to guide the Coys., to their quarters.

13. The working party of 1 N.C.O. and 10 men at DAYLIGHT CORNER will be relieved during the afternoon. They will hand over a list of all stores to the relieving Unit.

14. Completion of relief to be wired in CODE to Bn. H.Q.

(sgd) R. SMARTT,
2/Lieut & A/Adjt.,

SECRET.　　　　　　　RELIEF ORDERS　　　　　　F.321.
　　　　　　　　　　　　　by　　　　　　　　　23.10.16.
　　　　　　　Lt. Colonel F.S.N. Macrory,
　　　Commdg. 10th. (Service) Battn. Royal Inniskilling Fusiliers.

1. The Battalion will relieve the 14th. R. Irish Rifles in the Right Sub-Sector tomorrow.
   Relief not to commence before 4P.M.
2. Lewis Gunners, signallers and bombers will relieve at 1.30p.m. They must be marched as formed parties under an Officer or Senior N.C.O., they will leave Wakefield Huts at 12.30, and Transport Officer will have 1 double limber to carry these mens packs and proceed with them to Daylight Corner.
3. Coys. will move off at 3p.m. in the following order: C, D, B, and A. First Coy. will move off at 3 p.m. by platoons at 5 mins. interval. No movements to be over the open.
4. Route to be followed:- KINGSWAY TRENCH.
5. All Coys. will take over the same tactical dispositions which were in force in Coys. they relieve.
6. Coys. will take over Trench Stores, Log Books, Programmes of works and will forward a list of Trench Stores to reach this Office by 10a.m. sharp on the morning after relief.
7. Each Coy. will send up 1 Officer and 1 N.C.O. early to take over trenches.
8. Officers valises and spare kit to be taken to Qr. Masters Stores before 2 p.m.
   Officers Trench and Mess Kit to be taken to Qr. Masters Store and loaded on wagons detailed by Transport Officer.
   Officer's servants will remain with these Kits.
9. Rations will be at R.E. Farm at 6.45 p.m.
   Rations and Kit going to COOKER FARM will be brought up on separate Limber as formerly.
10. A certificate re. the cleanliness of huts etc. will be obtained from the 14th. R.I. Rifles (incoming Coys. of the) signed by an Officer Orderly Officer will remain behind and collect these.
11. Transport Lines will not be moved.
12. Lewis Gunners handcarts must not be used for carrying men's packs.
13. Men marched to the Trenches must be marched correctly as a formed party under an Officer, N.C.O., or Senior Soldier.
14. Transport Officer will arrange to have one double Limber per Coy. for men's packs.
    Report WAKEFIELD HUTS at 2.30 p.m., each limber alloted to a Coy. will follow behind the last Platoon of that Coy. as far as DAYLIGHT CORNER where each man will claim his own pack.
15. Completion of relief to be wired in code to Battn. Hd. Qrs.

　　　　　　　　　　(Signed) R. Smartt 2/Lt. & a/adjt.,
　　　　　　　　　　　　　10th. R. Innis. Fusrs.

CONFIDENTIAL.

W A R   D I A R Y

of

10th ROYAL INNISKILLING FUSILIERS,

from 1st November 1916 to 30th November 1916.

WAR DIARY
INTELLIGENCE SUMMARY.
(Erase heading not required.)

Army Form C. 2118.

Instructions regarding War Diaries and Intelligence Summaries are contained in F. S. Regs., Part II. and the Staff Manual respectively. Title pages will be prepared in manuscript.

Place	Date	Hour	Summary of Events and Information	Remarks and references to Appendices
	1/11/16		Battalion in occupation of trench at AIRCRAFT FARM and DERRY HUTS, furnishing working parties for work on sector of "Line" held by Brigade.	
	2/11/16 to 4/11/16		Nothing to report	
	5/11/16		Bn relieved 14th R Irish Rifles in the line on night of 5/6	
	5.11.16 6		a quiet tour, we had 3 men killed.	
	11.11.16		Bn withdrew to Wakefield Huts (M.29.e) into Divisional reserve	
	13.11.16		Bn marched to BAILLEUL, leaving camp at 11.30 a.m. arms were fitted in a accompanied by Divisional Band. men were marched to the cinema hall held outside the town & men were given by 38th Divisional where an excellent performance was given by the Follies after the Follies some excellent films were shown on the cinematograph. Tea was very kindly provided by the 110th Field Ambulance & the Bn fell in again & bn marched back to camp.	

Army Form C. 2118.

WAR DIARY
or
INTELLIGENCE SUMMARY.
(Erase heading not required.)

Place	Date	Hour	Summary of Events and Information	Remarks and references to Appendices
	11.11.16 -17.11.16		Fine weather during this period but very cold and frosty.	
	17.11.16 -23.11.16		B's relieved 14th R.H.R. in the line. This morning a bombardment of the enemy trenches in front of their sector was carried out by French mortars, covered by the Div. artillery. On stokes fired over 1512 rounds & the medium French mortars 700 rounds, doing considerable damage to the enemy trenches, wood & sandbags being sent flying in all directions. Enemy retaliation weak; what no casualties. This was the quietest tour we have had in this part of the line. presumably on account of SAXONS having come into the line opposite us. We had one man killed during the tour by a trench mortar. Witnessed this evening is DERRY HUTS (N.32 central).	AIRCRAFT FARM.
	24.11.16		From 10.30 p.m – 11.40 p.m enemy bombarded 11th Innis killing line very heavily. During this activity our guns were very active and about 12. 5.9 shrapnel burst round	AIRCRAFT FARM

WAR DIARY
or
INTELLIGENCE SUMMARY.

Army Form C. 2118.

Place	Date	Hour	Summary of Events and Information	Remarks and references to Appendices
	29.11.16		presumably searching for battery positions, several bullets came through some of the huts, but there were no casualties. Relieved 14th R IRISH RIFLES in the right subsector (N.36).	
	30.11.16	2 pm – 3.15 pm.	Our Trench mortars in 107th Brigade area subjected enemy trenches to a very heavy bombardment, enemy retaliation weak, he fired a few T.M's on us, no damage. 2nd Lieuts. BORCHERDS, BROWN, KEOGH and CRONIN left the Bn.	
	2.12.16		2nd Lt T. McKNIGHT joined the Bn to-day & 15 posted to C. Coy.	
	2.12.16		No. 16093. R.S.M WHITE A.] Awarded Military Medal " 15630. C.S.M IRWIN. R.S. " 15740. S/Sgt MILLS. E.P. " 7329u Pte ANDERSON. W	

Yn Macauly Lt Colonel.
Commdg 8th R Innis Fus

SECRET. RELIEF ORDERS. P. 331.
by 4.11.16.
Lieut-Colonel F.S.N. MACRORY,
Commanding 10th. Battalion Royal Inniskilling Fuslrs.

1. The Battalion will relieve the 14th. Royal Irish Rifles in the line to-morrow, 5th. inst. Relief not to begin before 3.30 p.m.

2. Lewis Gunners, Signallers, and Battalion Bombers will relieve at 2 p.m. They must be marched as formed parties under an officer, or senior N.C.O.

3. The route will be via KINGSWAY.

4. All movement will be by Platoons at 5 minutes interval. No movement will take place over the open.

5. Men marching to the trenches must be marched correctly as a formed party under an officer, N.C.O., or senior soldier.

6. Order of Relief:-
   "A" Coy. to right of Front Line.
   "B" "   " left "   "   "
   "C" "   " R. E. FARM.
   "D" "   " BATTLE HEADQUARTERS.

7. Companies will take over same tactical dispositions as are in force in Companies they relieved.

8. Companies will take over Trench Stores, Log Books, and programmes of Work. Lists of Trench Stores due at Battn. Headquarters by 11 a.m. on 6th. inst.

9. Completion of Relief to be wired to Battalion Headquarters in code.

10. All blankets to be ready at 10 a.m. to be taken to Quartermaster's Store. Cookers to be ready at 2.30 p.m. Orderly Room Boxes at 3 p.m. Officers Trench Kit and Mess Boxes at 4 p.m. Officers Spare Kit and Coys. Spare Kit at 12 noon.

11. Each Company will draw 20 pair of Gum Boots at DAYLIGHT CORNER on their way to the Trenches. Headquarters will draw 7 pair. Segt. Turner will draw 11 pair for party working in KINGSWAY.

12. Segt. Turner and 10 men will relieve same number of 14th. Royal Irish Rifles at DAYLIGHT CORNER as a working party on KINGSWAY.
    L/Cpl. Dalgleish "B" Coy. and 3 men will relieve control Post of 14th. Royal Irish Rifles at DAYLIGHT CORNER. Quartermaster will arrange to ration above.

13. The Battalion Orderly Officer will collect Certificates re Billets from incoming Unit (14th. Royal Irish Rifles).

1 Copy to Bde. Hd. Qrs.   8 Copy to Signalling Officer.
2 "   "   Bn. Hd. Qrs.   9 "   " Intelligence Officer.
3 "   "   C.O. 14th. R.Ir.R. 10 "   " Bombing Officer.
4 "   "   "A" Coy.   11 "   " Quartermaster.
5 "   "   "B" "   12 "   " Transport Officer.
6 "   "   "C" "   13 "   " File.
7 "   "   "D" "

                    (Signed)   C.N.L. STRONGE,
                                Captain & Adjutant.

F. 337.
11.11.16.

RELIEF ORDERS
- by -
Lieut-Colonel F. S. N. MACRORY,
Commanding 10th Battalion Royal Inniskilling Fusiliers.

1. The 14th Bn. Royal Irish Rifles will relieve the battalion in the right sub-sector of the trenches to-morrow - Relieving Unit will not pass DAYLIGHT CORNER before 4.30p.m.
   The battalion after relief will withdraw to WAKEFIELD Huts relieving the 11th Bn. Royal Innis., Fus.,

2. Lewis Gunners, Battalion Bombers and Signallers will relieve during the afternoon.

3. Route via KINGSWAY when possible.

4. All movement will be by platoons at 5 minutes interval

5. All parties must be marched as formed bodies under an officer, N.C.O. or senior soldier.

6. Transport Officer will arrange to send two double Limbers to R.E. Farm to take back packs belonging to "A" and "B" Coys.,   These Coys., will arrange to leave a man in charge of packs to help to load them.
   Two limbers to be at DAYLIGHT CORNER by 5 p.m. to take back packs of "C" and "D" Coys., which the men will load on to them as they pass.
   Coy Officers Kit and Mess Kit to be at R.E. Farm at 5 p.m.
   Headquarters Kit to be ready by 5.30 p.m. at COOKER FARM.   Officers Servants to remain with their Kit which will be brought back by Transport Of the 14th Royal Ir. Rif.

7. All trench stores and Log Books to be handed over to incoming Coys., also programmes of Work.

8. Completion of relief to be wired to Battalion Headquarters in CODE.

9. Platoons to hand over their Gum Boots to N.C.O. in charge of Drying Room at DAYLIGHT CORNER and obtain receipt for same.

10. Coy Commanders will see that men take their old pair of socks out with them.

Issued at 6 p.m.

(sgd) C.N.L. STRONGE,
Captain & Adjutant.

Copies to :-

1. 109th Brigade   2. O.C. 14th R. Irish Rif.
3. 11th Royal Innis., Fus., 4. Commanding Officer
5. O.C. "A" Coy.,   6. O.C. "B" Coy.,
7. O.C. "C" Coy.,   8. O.C. "D" Coy.,
9. Signalling Officer   10. Lewis Gun Officer.
11. FILE.

SECRET
Ref. Map 28 S.W.
1/20,000

16th. Nov., 1916.

Reference 109th. Brigade Order No.1.

R E L I E F   O R D E R S
- by -
Lieut-Colonel F.S.N. Macrory,
Commanding 10th. (S) Bn. Royal Inniskilling Fusiliers.

1. The 10th. Royal Inniskilling Fusiliers will relieve the 14th. Royal Irish Rifles in the right Sub Sector to-morrow, 17th. inst. Relieving Unit will not pass DAYLIGHT CORNER before 5 p.m.
The 14th. Royal Irish Rifles will withdraw into Divisional Reserve after relief, relieving the 10th. Royal Inniskilling Fusiliers.

2. Lewis Gunners, Signallers, and Battalion Bombers will relieve during the day. They must be marched as formed parties under an Officer or Senior N.C.O. They will not pass DAYLIGHT CORNER before 3 p.m. Transport Officer will have 2 Limbers at Orderly Room at 2 p.m. to take their Kits, Lewis Guns, etc. to DAYLIGHT CORNER. Lewis Gun Hand Carts will be handed over to Quartermaster.
The route will be via KINGSWAY.

3. All movements will be by platoons at 5 minutes interval. No movement will take place over the open.

4. Men marching to and from the trenches must be marched correctly as a formed party under an Officer, N.C.O. or Senior soldier.
Order of Relief:-
   "C" Coy. to Right Front Line.
   "D" "   " Left   "   "
   "A" "   " R.E. Farm.
   "B" "   " Mine Shafts.

5. Companies will take over the same tactical dispositions which were in force in the Battalion the relieve.

6. All Trench Stores, Log Books and programmes of Work will be taken over by relieving Companies. Lists will be forwarded so as to reach Battalion Headquarters before 11 a.m. on the day after relief.

7. Transport Officer will have 1 Limber per Company at Orderly Room at 3 p.m. to convey men's packs to DAYLIGHT CORNER.

8. All Officers spare kit to be at Quartermaster's Store by 2 p.m. Trench Kit and Mess Kit to be ready at 4 p.m. Officers servants will load this and accompany it to Trenches.

9. All blankets to be at Quartermaster's Store by 1 p.m.
Straw will be collected at 12 noon by Transport in Wagon.

10. Each Company will draw 20 pair of Gum Boots at DAYLIGHT CORNER on their way to the Trenches. Headquarters will draw 7 pair. Sgt. Turner 11 pair for party working on KINGSWAY, he will relieve party of 14th. Royal Irish Rifles at DAYLIGHT CORNER. One N.C.O. and 3 men will relieve Control post of 14th. Royal Irish Rifles at DAYLIGHT CORNER. Quartermaster will arrange to ration above party.

11. Battalion Orderly Officer will collect Certificates re Billets from Incoming Unit.

12. Completion of Reliefs to be wired <u>in code</u> to Bn. Headquarters.

(Signed) C.N.T. Stronge,

Issued at 9 p.m.   Captain & Adjutant.

Copies to:-

1. To 109th. Brigade.
2. To 14th. Royal Irish Rifles.
3. To O. C. 10th. Royal Innis. Fus.
4. To O. C. "A" Coy.
5. To O. C. "B" Coy.
6. To O. C. "C" Coy.
7. To O. C. "D" Coy.
8. To Quartermaster.
9. To Transport Officer.
10. To File.

14th BATTALION,
ROYAL IR. RIFLES.
No. RN 1676
Date 23.11.16

F. 350.
22.11.16.   No 2.

SECRET.
─────────────
Reference Map 28 S.W. 1/20,000
                                    109th Brigade Order No. 2.
───

RELIEF ORDERS
- by -
Lieut-Colonel F. S. N. MACRORY,
Commanding 10th Bn. Royal Inniskilling Fusiliers.
* * * * * * * * *

1.   The Battalion will be relieved by the 14th Bn. Royal
Ir. Rif., in the Right Sub Sector to-morrow 23rd inst.,
        Relieving Unit not to pass DAYLIGHT CORNER before
5 p.m.
        The Battalion, after relief will withdraw into
Brigade Reserve, relieving the 11th Bn. Royal Inniskilling
Fusiliers at DERRY HUTS.

2.   Lewis Gunners, Signallers and Bn. Bombers will relieve
at 3 p.m.   These must be marched as formed parties under
an Officer or Senior N.C.O.

3.   The route will be via KINGSWAY.

4.   All movements will be by platoons at 5 minutes
interval.   No movement will take place over the open.

5.   Men marching and- to and from the trenches must be
marched correctly as a formed party under an Officer, N.C.O.
or Senior Soldier, and all tendency to straggle (which is
still noticeable in these small parties) checked.

6.   All Coys., will take over the same tactical dispositions
which were in force in the Coys., they relieve.

7.   All Trench Stores, Log Books and programmes of work
will be handed over to Relieving Coys.,

8.   R.E. Working Parties now found by the 11th Bn. R.
Innis., Fus., will cease after work on the night of
22/23rd inst., and will be found on the night of the 24th
by the 10th Bn. Royal Innis., Fus.,

9.   All Coy., and Mess Kit, and Officers Kits to be at
R.E. FARM by 5 p.m.   HEADQUARTERS KIT at COOKER FARM at
5.30 p.m.   Officers servants will remain with Kit.

10. Battalion Orderly Officer (2/Lieut R. SMARTT) will
take over DERRY CAMP at 3 p.m.

11. Completion of relief to be wired in code to Battalion
Headquarters.

                            (sgd) C.N.L. STRONGE,
                                    Captain & Adjutant.

ISSUED AT S.E.H.

Copies to:-
1. 109th Brigade.   2. 14th R. Ir. Rif.   3. 11th R. Innis. Fus
4. Commanding Officer   5. O"C" "A" Coy.,   6. O.C. "B" Coy.,
7. O.C. "C" Coy.,   8. O.C. "D" Coy.,   9. Quartermaster
10. Transport Officer   11. R.S.M.   12. Bombing Officer
13. Sniping Officer   14. Lewis Gun Officer   15. Signalling Off.,
16. F I L E.

SECRET. Copy No. 2
RELIEF ORDERS. 28.11.16.
-by-
Lieut. Colonel F.S.N. MACRORY,
Commdg., 10th. Battn. Royal Inniskilling Fusiliers.

1. The 10th. R.Innis. Fus. will relieve the 14th. R. Ir. Rifles in the Right Sub-Sector on Wednesday 29th. instant.
Relieving Unit not to pass DAYLIGHT CORNER before 4 p.m.
The 14th. R. Ir. Rifles after relief will withdraw into Brigade Reserve relieving the 10th. R. Innis. Fus.

2. Lewis Gunners, Signallers, Battn. Bombers and Scouts will relieve at 3.45 p.m. They must be marched as formed parties under an Officer or Senior N.C.O.

3. The route for the Right Sub Sector will be Kingsway.

4. All movements will be by Platoons at 5 minutes interval.

5. Men marching to and from the trenches must be marched as a formed party under an Officer, N.C.O. or Senior Soldier, and all tendency to straggle (which is still noticeable in these small parties) checked.

6. All Coys. will take over the same tactical dispositions which were in force in the Coys. they relieve.

7. All Trench Stores, Log Books and programmes of work will be taken over by the Relieving Units. Lists will be forwarded to reach Battn. Headquarters before noon on the day after relief.

8. R.E. Working Parties now found by the 10th. R. Innis. Fus, will cease after work on the night of the 28/29 th. instant, and will be found on the night of the 30th. by the 14th. R. Ir. Rifles.

9. Completion of relief to be wired in Code to Battalion Headquarters.

10. Straw will be tied up and left in Corner of huts.

11. Blankets to be ready for Transport to Q.M. Stores at 10 am., also Officer's spare Kit and Company Kits. Orderly Room and Officer's Mess Kit boxes will be ready at 2.30 p.m.
Officer's Trench Kit at 4 p.m.
Officer's Servants will accompany these to the Trenches.

12. 2/Lt. Starr will hand over all Company and Headquarter Billets to incoming Battalion.

Sgd. C.N.L. STRONGE Capt. & Adjt.,
10th. Battn. R.Innis. Fus.

Copies to-
1. 109th. Brigade.
2. 14th. R.Ir. Rifles.
3. Commanding Officer.
4. O.C."A" Coy.
5. O.C."B" Coy.
6. O.C."C" Coy.
7. O.C."D" Coy.
8. Quartermaster.
9. Transport Officer.
10. R.S.M.
11. Bombing Officer.
12. Sniping Officer.
13. Lewis Gun Officer.
14. File.

C O N F I D E N T I A L

W A R   D I A R Y

of

10th BATTALION ROYAL INNISKILLING FUSILIERS

from

1st December 1916

to

31st December 1916

10th R. INNIS: FUS:

PAGE I.

Army Form C. 2118.

WAR DIARY
or
INTELLIGENCE SUMMARY.
(Erase heading not required.)

Instructions regarding War Diaries and Intelligence Summaries are contained in F. S. Regs, Part II. and the Staff Manual respectively. Title pages will be prepared in manuscript.

Place	Date	Hour	Summary of Events and Information	Remarks and references to Appendices
	December 1916. 5th		The Battalion was relieved in the SPANBROEK sector on the afternoon of the 5th inst: by the 6th Bn. The CONNAUGHT RANGERS (16th Div-) after relief the Bn. withdrew to DERRY CAMP (M.36. central) into Brigade reserve.	N.S.
	6th		Bn. moved from DERRY CAMP to KORTEPYP CAMP via NEUVE EGLISE, into Divisional Reserve, being relieved at DERRY CAMP by the 7th LEINSTERS (16th Division).	N.S.
	6-13th		Bn. remained during this period in Divisional Reserve at KORTEPYP.	N.S.
	13th		On the 13th the Battalion relieved the 11th R. INNIS. FUS. in the Brigade right subsector, which had been taken over from the 25th Division on the 5th inst by the 11th R. INNIS. FUS.	N.S.
	13-21st		A very quiet period indeed and no casualties were suffered. Patrols were out every night, 2 German patrols were seen, but one of which bombed a patrol under 2nd Lt. W.E. GRIFFITHS, which	N.S.

1577 Wt. W10791/1773 500,000 1/15 D. D. & L. A.D.S.S./Form/C. 2118.

10th R. INNIS. FUS.

PAGE III.

Army Form C. 2118.

WAR DIARY
or
INTELLIGENCE SUMMARY.

(Erase heading not required.)

Place	Date	Hour	Summary of Events and Information	Remarks and references to Appendices
	10th		Without horses without suffering any casualties. 25th Divisional artillery covered the Bde during this time. On the 10th inst. a draft of 53 men & one officer was received by the Battalion, 18 of them were cavalrymen (11th 8th & 13th Hussars)	elis.
	18th		The officer Major S.J. SOMERVILLE saw service in GALLIPOLI with the 1st Bn R. INNIS. FUS. Lieut (a/capt) G.H. WEBB proceeded home 15 day under orders to report at FINNER CAMP (Authority 36th Div. letter 10/19.A. of. 8/12/16 J.)	elis.
			Major S.J. SOMERVILLE posted temporary to 14th R. Irish Rifles as 2nd in Command.	elis.
	19th		2/Lt. J. McMEEHAN joined the Battalion, & was posted to "D" coy. He had previously seen service with 5th R. IN. FUS.	elis.
			During this month No.15313 H/c. BELL R.J. "D" coy. No. 29444 " STEWART. " A coy. No. 16054 " THOMPSON. " A coy. proceeded to LONDON to undergo a course of instruction for Cadets.	

PLOEGSTEERT WOOD
U.19.C. 28.85. (Map ref 28 S.W.4)

10th R. INNIS. FUS.   PAGE III.

Army Form C. 2118.

WAR DIARY
or
INTELLIGENCE SUMMARY.
(Erase heading not required.)

Place	Date	Hour	Summary of Events and Information	Remarks and references to Appendices
PLOEGSTEERT WOOD.	21st		During DECEMBER 3 officers and 47 O.R.s were sent on leave the officers being MAJOR R.S. KNOX, 2nd Lieuts: RITTER & SWANN.	Wils.
			(RSO WILKINS) into Brigade Reserve into the GALLERIES at HYDE PARK CORNER. These galleries, which are tunnelled out of the side of HILL 63, accomodate at least 2 B'ns in bunks which are built along the sides of these underground streets, the whole is lit by electric light.	Wils.
	23rd		Capt. PICKEN R.A.M.C. returned from a course at medical HAZEBROUCK During his absence (17th-23rd) Capt. MUIR R.A.M.C. 110th F.A. Ambulance, was attached as M.O.	Wils.
	24th		Lt. Col. F.S.N. MACRORY proceeded to 2nd Army School of Instruct at WISQUES No STOMER for a conference of Commanding	Wils.

10th R. Innis. Fus.

PAGE IV

Army Form C. 2118.

WAR DIARY
or
INTELLIGENCE SUMMARY.
(Erase heading not required.)

Place	Date	Hour	Summary of Events and Information	Remarks and references to Appendices
	25th		Officers having one week. Christmas Day passed very quietly, the men were given a large feed in the middle of the day consisting of 3 pigs, plum pudding, apples, oranges, beer etc.; in the afternoon companies had concerts & Capt. PATON C.F. shewed his cinematograph owing to the limited amount of room the concerts were small but the men enjoyed their day. In the evening a Battalion dinner was held in the CATACOMBS & was a great success. 2nd Lt. S.S. RICHARDS joined 109th T.M. Battery (STOKES) During December the following officers attended courses of instruction as follows. 2nd Lieut. R.B.N.SMARTT.] 36th Div. 2/Lieut. G.L. Ritter 2nd Army Bombing G. NELSON.] School. School (TERDEGHEM)	App. App.

Place BACEGSTEET
Map ref 28.S.W.t.23.34
1/10,000
26th

10th R. INNIS. FUS.

PAGE IV

WAR DIARY
or
INTELLIGENCE SUMMARY
(Erase heading not required)

Army Form C. 2118.

Place	Date	Hour	Summary of Events and Information	Remarks and references to Appendices
PLOEGSTEERT Map 28.S.W.4 Edition 5d 1/10,000	December 29th		Lieut. E. CRAWLEY Div: anti-gas School. CAPT. A.F.COOK. Lewis gun School Le TOUQUET. 2nd Lt. R.J. FANNING. 2nd Army School of signalling. Col. L.S. RACROFT. 2nd Army central school (commanding officers course) The Battalion took over the Brigade front — relieving the 11th R. INNIS. FUS. in the right sector & the 14th R. Irish Rifles in the left sector. Battalion front now runs from U.14 b.95.40. to U.8 a.45.25 Battalion Head Quarters remain at KIMAVADY LODGE (U.14 a.90.90)	A.I.S. A.I.S.
	31st		Our Heavy artillery bombarded MESSINES between the following hours 10 p.m. – 10.10 p.m. 11 p.m. – 11.10 p.m. midnight – 12.10 a.m. enemy retaliated a/c last bombardment, but caused little damage. Lieut. K.A. McKENZIE rejoined the Bn. 65th day. He was wounded on 1/7/16.	A.I.S.
	28th		Lieut. J. McCAW joined the Bn & was posted to "C coy." He has previously served in this country in the 2nd COUNTY of LONDON YEOMANRY.	A.I.S.

Funucourf. Lieut: Colonel.
Comdg. 10th R. INNIS. FUS.

SECRET.
No. 2.

F 567.
28.12.16.

by
Major R.S. Knox, Commanding 10th. R. Innis. Fusrs.

1. The battalion will relieve the 11th. Buttn. R. INNIS. Fus. in the right Sub Sector and the 14th. R.Ir. Rifles in the Left Sub Sector to-morrow 29th. Decr. Relief to commence after 2 p.m.

2. Forts STABLE, CHATEAU and WRIGGS will be taken over by 11th. R. Innis. Fus. and FORT SLATES by 14th. R.Ir. Rifles at mid-day.

3. C Company will relieve front line Company of 11th. Bn. Royal Innis. Fusiliers.
D Company will relieve front-line Company 14th. Royal Irish Rifles.
A Company will relieve company of 11th. R. Royal Innis. Fus. at HALF WAY HOUSE with 2 platoons and the company of 11th. R.I.F. at ASHER HOUSE. Each platoon to take over tactical disposition of 2 platoons of the 11th. Royal Innis. Fus.
B Company will send 1 platoon to relieve platoon of 14th. R.I.R. in REGINA CUTOFF, and 1 platoon to relieve platoon in Locality 3 taking over stores : same tactical disposition. The remaining 2 platoons of the Company will take over from Company of 14th Royal I.R. in subsidiary line 7. ROSSIGNOL to MESSINES ROAD. Company Headquarters at DEAD COW FARM. One platoon to take over tactical dispositions of each 2 platoons of 14th. Royal Irish Rif. Scouts, Snipers, and Battalion Bombers will go to HALF WAY HOUSE and be attached to "A" company for Rations.

(4) Lewis Gunners, Bombers and Signallers will commence relief at 12.30.
(5) Companies relieving 11th. Royal Innis. Fus. will do VIA ANSCROFT AVENUE. and those relieving 14th. Royal I.R. by GAS TRENCH.
(6) All movements will be by Platoons at 200 yards interval. Men marching from the trenches must be marched correctly as a formed party under an Officer, N.C.O. or senior soldier.
(7) Battalion in the line will have guides at HYDE PARK CORNER at 2pm.
(8) Each Company will send 1 Officer and 1 N.C.O. to take over stores etc., during the morning, they will also take over work in hand.
(9) 2/Lt.S.GRIFFITHS will hand over billets in CATACOMBS to 11th Royal Innis. Fus. and will obtain certificates for same.
(10) "A" and "B" Coys. blankets to be ready for Transport at 9am. a loading party to be detached detailed by Companies.
"C" and "D" to be ready at 11am. and loading parties to be detailed also.
Headquarters will take the blankets to LIMAVADY LODGE.
Officers spare kits and mess kit to be ready at 2.30pm.
(11) Lists of trench stores taken over to be returned to this office by noon 30th. inst.
(12) Companies will take up with them at least 12 pairs of gum boots per company.
(13) Transport lines will not be moved.
(14) Completion of relief to be wired incode to Battalion Headquarters

(1) 109th. Brigade
(2) 14th. Royal I.R.
(3) 11th. Royal Innis. Fus.
(4) C.O.
(5) O.C. "A" Coy.
(6) O.C. "B" Coy.
(7) O.C. "C" Coy.
(8) O.C. "D" Coy.
(9) R.S.M.
(10) Transport Officer.
(11) Quartermaster.
(12) Lewis Gun Officer.
(13) Signal Officer.
(14) Bombing Officer.
(15) File.

C.N.L.STRONGE,
Captain and Adjutant,
10th. Bn. Royal Innis. Fus.

TRENCH STORE LIST. TAKEN OVER BY............FROM............

GAS APPARATUS.

AMMONIA CAPSULES (TINS)	HORNS KLAXON
AMMONIA TUBES	HELMETS GAS
BLANKETS ANTI-GAS	SALVUS BREATHING SETS
FLAPPER FANS	SYRINGES
GONGS	SOLUTION JARS
GAS TESTER	VERMORAL SPRAYER & SOLUTION
HORNS STOMBOS	VACUUM BULBS
HORNS TENOR	

TRENCH CAMP EQUIPMENT.

BOOTS GUM THIGH	LOG BOOKS
BUCKETS LATRINE	LAMP HURICANE
BEDS CAMP	LAMPS (OIL)
BRAZIERS	MEAT SAFES
BROOMS	MEGAPHONES
BARROWS	PERISCOPES
BASINS WASHING	RODS MEASURING
BOILERS	SOYERS STOVES
DIXIES CAMP	STICKS MICROPHONE
FOOD CONTAINERS	STRETCHERS (TRENCH)
FIRE EXTINGUISHERS	STRETCHERS (SITTING)
GRINDSTONES	TUBS WASHING
LANTERNS FOLDING	TABLES
LADDERS	WEATHER COCKS

R.E. STORES.

AXES	RAMMERS
BILL HOOKS	SHOVELS
HAMMERS	SAWS
HOOKS REAPING	SICKLES
MALLETS	SCRAPERS (MUD)
MAULS	SCOOPS WATER
CROWBARS	TAPES MEASURING
PLATES LOOPHOLE	TAPES TRACING
PICKS	TRUCKS HAND
PUMPS & HOSE	

TRENCH AMMUNITION & BOMBS ETC.

BOMBS (STOKES)	ROCKETS RED
BOMBS (SMOKE)	GREEN
MSK BOMBS	WHITE
DETONATORS NO.8 MK.VII	ROCKET STICKS
GRENADES (BOMBS) NO. 5	ROCKET STANDS
NO. 3	VERY LIGHTS 1"D.I.
NEWTON	1½"D.I.
NO.23	RED
NO.19	GREEN

TACTICAL EQUIPMENT.

CATAPULTS	LEWIS GUN (STANDS
COSTUMES CAMOUFLAGE	RIFLE RESTS FIXED
COSTUMES SNIPERS	RIFLE BATTERIES
COSTUMES ACID PROOF	RANGE CARDS
DAGGERS	RIFLES FITTED TO BATTERIES
ARTILLERY	SNIPERSCOPES (RIFLE)
GUNS (WEST SPRING)	SWIVELS MOUNTING
RIFLE GRENADE STANDS	SNIPERS DUMMIES
INDUCTION BUZZERS	SCREEN POSTS
KNOBKERRIES	VEILS OBSERVERS

TRENCH RESERVE RATIONS & WATER.

BARRELS	PETROL TINS
BISCUITS (BOXES)	TANKS
IRON RATIONS (COMPLETE)	TINNED BEEF (BOXES)
JARS	
RIFLES FOR RIFLE BATTERIES (NOT BULGED)	STOVES OIL DRUM
RIFLES FOR RIFLE GRENADES (BULGED)	STOVES PRIMUS
CONTAINERS FOOD HOT	ALIDADES PERISCOPIC
STOVES SMALL DOUBLE DOORS	ALIDADES TELESCOPIC

Handed over
Rank & Name..........................
Unit..........................
Date.......... Received
Rank & Name..........................
Unit..........................

CONFIDENTIAL.

WAR DIARY

of

10th ROYAL INNISKILLING FUSILIERS

from

1st January 1917

to

31st January 1917

Reference Map
PLOEGSTEERT 28. S.W. Edition 4.A.
Scale 1/10,000

10th R. INNIS: FUS:
WAR DIARY

Page I
Army Form C. 2118.

Place	Date	Hour	Summary of Events and Information	Remarks and references to Appendices
	January 1917. 1st		Artillery active on both sides during the day, two men being killed by a shell near the barricade on the PLOEGSTEERT — MESSINES road. 2nd. Lieut: R.M. BOYLE joined the Battalion to-day. He had previously seen service with 1st Bn R. INNIS. FUS. being wounded with them in JULY. He is posted to "C. company".	e.U.S.
	2nd		2nd Lieut: H.C. BEALE joined the Battalion to-day from 12th Bn. R. INNIS. FUS: and is posted to "B company."	e.U.S.
	4th		A fighting patrol of 16 O.R. and 2 officers was sent out to try and intercept any German patrols that might be out. None were seen, but we had one man killed being struck in the chest by a stray bullet.	e.U.S.
	6th		11th Bn R. INNIS. FUS: relieved the Battalion in the line during the afternoon. Bn withdrew into Brigade Reserve in the CATACOMBS at HYDE PARK CORNER relieving the 11th INNIS. FUS. 2nd Lieut: T. BROWN joined the Bn to-day and is posted to D company.	e.U.S.

Reference map.
PLOEGSTEERT. 28. S.W. Edit. 4.A.
Scale 1/10,000

10th R. INNIS. FUS.

WAR DIARY
—
INTELLIGENCE SUMMARY.
(Erase heading not required.)

Army Form C. 2118.

Place	Date	Hour	Summary of Events and Information	Remarks and references to Appendices
PLOEGSTEERT WOOD. HYDE PARK CORNER, U.19.6.30.80.	January 1917. 7th.		Working parties in the line commenced at 4 p.m. to day.	aulf.
	8th.		Divis. [Divisional] pioneers were firing on range all day. Working parties.	aulf.
	9th–13th		" " nothing unusual occurred during this time.	aulf.
	14th		Battalion relieved the 11th R. INNIS. FUS. in the line.	aulf.
	15.16.		quiet.	
	17th		Our artillery shelled enemy trenches & MESSINES from 4.50 p.m – 5 p.m. 2nd Lt. T. SWANN was wounded in the stomach by shrapnel.	aulf.
	19th		2nd Lt: C. K. KEVIN joined Bn to day, and is posted to B company. He previously served with the 10th (Reserve) Bn R.Ir. Fus.	aulf.
	20th		Enemy artillery and Trench Mortars very active. 3 men in D company were killed by a T.M., & one wounded.	aulf.
	21st		Enemy artillery still fairly active.	aulf.
	22nd		Hostile Bombardment of our trenches from 1.45 p.m – 7.15 p.m. very severe on the right round ANTON'S FARM; the relief shals of commenced at 2.p.m. but owing to activity was not completed until 10.45.p.m. when Bn withdrew into Brigade reserve at the Catacombs.	aulf.

1577 Wt. W10791/1773 500,000 1/15 D. D. & L.   A.D.S.S./Forms/C. 2118.

Reference Map
Ploegsteert 28.S.W. edition 4.A.
Scale 1/10,000

10th R. INNIS: FUS.

PART III.
Army Form C. 2118.

WAR DIARY
or
INTELLIGENCE SUMMARY
(Erase heading not required.)

Place	Date	Hour	Summary of Events and Information	Remarks and references to Appendices
	January.			
	24th		We were extremely lucky in only having 2 men wounded during this shelling.	
			2nd Lieut. S. MARK and 2nd Lieut R.C. HUGHES reported to-day on transfer from 7th R. Innis. Fus., and are posted to B and A coys. respectively.	aaa.
	29th		2nd Lt. H.D.F.O. NOBLE reported to-day from 15th motor machine gun battery and is posted to C company.	aaa.
	30th		Battalion relieved 11th R. Innis. Fus. in the line.	aaa.
	31st		Day quiet. Had hostile m.g. which started on 14th inst. still continues. Slight fall of snow last night.	aaa.
			During this month 74 men went on leave, and 3 officers, namely Lt. E. CRAWLEY, Hon. Lt. & Qr. Master G.G. KENDALL and 2nd Lt. T. Mc COX.	
			During this month the following officers attended courses:— a/Capt. W.J.K. MOON. Lewis gun course LE TOUQUET 4.1.17 – 11.1.17. Lieut. K.A. McKENZIE. Sniping course GODEWAERSVELDE. 6.1.17. 14.1.17. 2/Lt. J. McCAW. ⎫ Div. School SteMARIE CAPPEL. 7.1.17 – 31.1.17. 2/Lt. N. McMEECHAN. ⎭	aaa.

PLOEGSTEERT

Reference map.
PLOEGSTEERT. 28. S.W. Edition 4.A. Scale 1/10,000

10th R. INNIS. Fus.

WAR DIARY
INTELLIGENCE SUMMARY

Army Form C. 2118.

Place	Date	Hour	Summary of Events and Information	Remarks and references to Appendices
	January.		Courses. 2nd Lt. H.C. BEALE 2nd army signalling school ZUYTPEENE 15.1.17 — Feb:	
			2nd Lt. R.M. BOYLE Div: anti-gas school 21.1.17 — 25.1.17.	W.S.
			2nd Lt. J.G. NELSON 2nd army stokes mortar course TERDEGHEM 22.1.17 — 28.1.17.	
			2nd Lt. T. McKNIGHT Div: Bombing school 31.12.16 — 13.1.17.	

Lumsbury.
Lt. Col.
Comdg. 10th R. Innis. Fus.

PLOEGSTEERT WOOD

WAR DIARY

of

10th BATTALION ROYAL INNIS. FUSILIERS.

From 1st February 1917
To 28th February 1917

Page 1

Lt. R. INNIS. FUS.

MAP Reference
PLOEGSTEERT.
28. S.W.4. Edition 4 A.
Scale 1/10,000

WAR DIARY
INTELLIGENCE SUMMARY
(Erase heading not required.)

Army Form C. 2118.

Place	Date	Hour	Summary of Events and Information	Remarks and references to Appendices
	February 1st		Lt. Col. F.S.N. Macrory D.S.O. proceeded on 3 weeks leave, command of Battalion being taken over by Major R.S. Knot D.S.O. Capt. J.G. Pater proceeded on leave. A certain amount of Trench mortar and artillery activity on both sides throughout the day. Enemy aircraft very active.	A.W.S.
	2nd		Artillery fairly active during the day.	A.W.S.
	3rd		A quiet day.	A.W.S.
	4th		do.	A.W.S.
	5th		We bombarded enemy lines with artillery and T.M's between 2.30 p.m. and 3.30.p.m. in conjunction with 25th Division. Aircraft on both sides active. We had 1 Man Killed and 3 wounded.	A.W.S.
	6th		Day quiet, aircraft active on both sides.	A.W.S.
	7th		11th R. INNIS. FUS. relieved the Battalion in the line, the B'n withdrawing in 6 Brigade reserve at the GALLERIES HYDE PARK CORNER.	A.W.S.
	8th		Working parties in the lines commenced this evening.	A.W.S.

U.19.a.&.b. V.8. & Q.14.
PLOEGSTEERT WOOD.

MAP REFERENCE.
PLOEGSTEERT.
28.S.W. Edition 4.A.
Scale 1/10,000

10th R. INNIS. FUS:

WAR DIARY
—
INTELLIGENCE SUMMARY

Page II.
Army Form C. 2118.

Place	Date	Hour	Summary of Events and Information	Remarks and references to Appendices
	February 9th		Working parties.	AAA
	10th		Draft of 13.O.R. reported for duty to-day.	AAA
	11th		2nd Lt. H.T. JAMIESON having reported for duty from 1st R. INNIS. Fus. to-day, is taken on the strength of the Bn and posted 18th Company.	AAA
	12th 13th 14th		Working parties went.	AAA
	15th		At 1 a.m. a warning of 14th Bn "Stand to" on account of a heavy bombardment on left of Brigade front, but we did not have to move. The Battalion relieved the 11th R. Innis. Fus. in the front line. At 5 p.m. to-day a German aeroplane, a single decker HALBERSTADTER came down in our lines at U 14 C. 30.80, just in front of La HUTTE CHATEAU. The pilot was uninjured and surrendered to some men in C company. # It appeared that he had been up testing the engine, when he says he at once went to the shelter of the ALBATROSS but was hit by shrapnel from our A.A. guns when at 10,000 feet and had to come down. He was a corporal and had been an	AAA

PLOEGSTEERT WOOD
U. 19. a. 4. 6.   U. 8   and U. 14.

Map reference
PLOEGSTEERT.
28.S.W.4.
Edition 4.A. Scale 1/10,000

Page III.
Army Form C. 2118.

10th R./NN'15: FUS:

WAR DIARY
and
INTELLIGENCE SUMMARY.
(Erase heading not required.)

Place	Date	Hour	Summary of Events and Information	Remarks and references to Appendices
	16th		Instruction at various aviation schools.	
	17th		The plane was intact, with the exception of broken wheels, & a hole in the petrol tank, so after dark a party of men got it pulled out of the field and down the PLOEGSTEERT - MESSINES road to near HYDE PARK CORNER. The flying Corps sent a party during the night and took the plane away. About an hour after the plane came down hostile artillery was active apparently searching for the plane, but very few shells went near it. Enemy artillery & T.M.s fairly active.	W/S
	18th		Raid carried out on front of Brigade on our right at this morning. Bombardment began at 10.40 a.m. lasting for 1 hour, 1st Wilts & 10th Cheshires took part in the raid which was fairly successful. No. 15847 L/c. McGREGOR B company was killed by a shell this morning. Artillery on both sides active during the day. A message dropped by a German aeroplane was picked up by s- Sar by a man in a shell hole, it was tied up in a small bag weighted with sand, and a long streamer coloured Black, white and Red attached to it.	W/S

Map reference.
PLOEGSTEERT
28.S.W.4.
Edition 4A
Scale 1/10000

10th R. INNIS: FUS.

Page IV.

Army Form C. 2118.

WAR DIARY
or
INTELLIGENCE SUMMARY.
(Erase heading not required.)

Place	Date	Hour	Summary of Events and Information	Remarks and references to Appendices
	19th		The message stated that 2 of our airmen had been captured, one wounded, & that he was going on well. There has at least set in, it is a slow ground thaw, and the trenches are keeping fairly good. Day quiet.	
	20th		Day quiet. 2/Lt. Boyce joined to-day for duty and was posted to "B" Coy	W.S.
	21st		We carried out a raid this evening at 7.30 p.m. on enemy trenches in U.15.a. Strength of party 38 O.R. and 2 officers, (2nd Lt. W.C. GRIFFITHS in charge of party, and 2/Lt. T. McKNIGHT.) Our artillery opened at 7.30 p.m. on enemy trenches in U.9.C. and at 7.45 p.m. they switched over on to U.15.a. forming a box barrage, at the same time 12 stokes guns opened a portion of line that was to be raided, the stokes barrage lasted for 5 minutes and then the party, which had been lying out in "no man's land" during the bombardment, moved forward on the German trenches. They got in alright without having to use their Bangalore torpedoes.	W.S.

Map reference
Ploegsteert
28.S.W.4 Edition 4.A.
Scale 1/10000

10th R. WNS. FUS.

Page V.

Army Form C. 2118.

WAR DIARY
INTELLIGENCE SUMMARY
(Erase heading not required.)

Place	Date	Hour	Summary of Events and Information	Remarks and references to Appendices
	22nd		as the wire had been well cut, but 2nd Lt Griffiths finding the German trench filled with wire and being unable to make any progress, withdrew his men back to our trenches. Our casualties were, 2/Lt. McKNIGHT. Killed. 2nd Lt. 8 R. IFF 1748 wounded, (in the arm slight), and 5. O.R.s slightly wounded. These casualties were all caused by one hostile T.M. which was fired just after the party had left our own trenches. 2/Lt. McKNIGHT was hit in the head and killed instantaneously, he is a great loss to the Battalion. He was a most excellent bombing officer, and very good on patrols. Quiet Day.	Nil.
	23rd		Enemy bombarded our lines in V.14.b. from 5.50.a.m - 6.30.a.m. a large number of T.M's (large. medium & small) being used. He at the same time bombarded the Bn on our right. About 6.15 a.m. a party of Germans were seen by a No. 13. Platoon Lewis Gun team approaching our trenches under cover of the mist, which was very thick at this time. The gun at once opened fire and dispersed the	Nil.

10th R. INNIS. FUS.

WAR DIARY
INTELLIGENCE SUMMARY

Page VI.
Army Form C. 2118.

Place	Date	Hour	Summary of Events and Information	Remarks and references to Appendices
			park. When the gun opened on them a lot of shooting was heard, but results could not be observed. During this time another hostile patrol had entered the trenches by the B2. on our right but were very soon driven out again leaving 1 dead Boche behind. A great amount of ammunition was expended by the enemy, but this shoot was not SOS and our trenches were very slightly damaged. We had no casualties. The 11th R. INNIS. FUS. relieved the Bn this afternoon, & we withdrew in to the GALLERIES HYDEPARK CORNER in to Bde Reserve.	
	24th			
	25th		Bn. Battle in Div: Battle Near NEUVE EGLISE. A draft of 24 men joined Bn. 15 Jan from 2/26 City of London Regt. 11th R. INNIS. FUS. relieved the B2. at the GALLERIES, & we withdrew to BULFORD CAMP (T.20.c.4.1) into Divisional Reserve.	Apps. Apps.
	26th		Bn. relieving 9th R. Irish Rifles. This Brigade having now been relieved by the 107th Brigade, is withdrawn in to Divisional Reserve for 1 month. Lieut. E. CRAWLEY died of heart failure this morning, he had been	Apps.

Page VII

WAR DIARY
INTELLIGENCE SUMMARY

Place	Date	Hour	Summary of Events and Information	Remarks and references to Appendices
BULFORD CAMP T.20.C.4.1.	27th		sent to WESTHOF FARM to select a field for a battalion parade and it appears that just before he got to the farm he had a sudden fit & died before any medical help could be obtained. Bn. turning up till 1 p.m. afternoon recreational training, i.e. football, cross country, bayonet etc. training for inter-Battalion competition to be held at the end of the month next.	A.W.S.
	28th		Same at on 27th inst. Lieut. E. CRAWLEY was buried with full military honours in the BAILLEUL cemetery at 3 p.m. to-day. Capt. W. J. K. non was in charge of firing party (40 men) & 4 buglers taken from the late Lt. CRAWLEY'S platoon. 1 Officer and 7 O.R's proceeded on leave during this month. A draft of 49 O.R.s arrived to-day from 6th London Regt.	A.W.S.

W. McGeagh. Lt. Col.
28.2/17. con.tg. 10th R. INNIS. FUS:

CONFIDENTIAL.

WAR DIARY

of

10th BATTALION ROYAL INNIS. FUSILIERS,

from 1st March 1917
to 31st March 1917.

Army Form C. 2118.

WAR DIARY
of
INTELLIGENCE SUMMARY. 10th Bn. R. Innis. Fus.

(Erase heading not required.)

Instructions regarding War Diaries and Intelligence Summaries are contained in F. S. Regs., Part II. and the Staff Manual respectively. Title pages will be prepared in manuscript.

Place	Date	Hour	Summary of Events and Information	Remarks and references to Appendices
Bulford Camp	1/3/17		The Battalion is still in Divisional Reserve. The time is occupied by training in the forenoon & Recreational training (football, boxing etc) in the Afternoon.	
do	2/3/17		This is our day at the Divisional Baths (DRANOUTRE), so that the training is curtailed a little. The good weather still continued.	
do	3/3/17		6 O.Rs. returned today from Divisional Signal School as qualified Signallers.	
do	4/3/17		2nd Lieut. P. PICKEN and 2nd Lieut. W.P. JOHNSTON arrived with the Battalion and were posted to "D" and "A" Coys respectively. 2nd Lieut. R.B.N. SMARTT left for LONDON today, to complete his Medical Studies and was accordingly struck off the Battalion Strength. 34 ORs joined today from 12th Res Battn. R. Innis. Fus.	
do	5/3/17		"A" Company was at CLANDEBOYE Range this forenoon.	
do	9/3/17		23H21 Lce. Cpl. H.G. Irwin proceeded to Base today for disposal as under age.	

Army Form C. 2118.

WAR DIARY
or
INTELLIGENCE SUMMARY. 10th Bn. R. Innis. Fus.

(Erase heading not required.)

Place	Date	Hour	Summary of Events and Information	Remarks and references to Appendices
Buford Camp.	10/3/17		"A" & "B" Companies proceeded to KEMMEL to dig trenches etc. They had dinner out and returned about 5 pm.	
do —	11/3/17		"C" & "D" Companies went to KEMMEL today.	
do —	12/3/17		2nd Lieut. S. E. RICHARDS has been transferred to ENGLAND "Sect". Lieut. H. T. ALLON being employed as P.B. Officer in V Army is struck off the strength of the Battalion. "A" & "B" Companies went to KEMMEL. No. 13397 C.S.M. Campbell H.M. has been taken on Home Establishment, and 16010 A/C.S.M. has been appointed C.S.M. and promoted W.O. Class II wd from 28.2.17. SCOTT E.	
do —	13/3/17		"C" & "D" Companies proceeded for duty to KEMMEL.	
do —	15/3/17		The Champion Platoon of the Battalion (No. 15 "D" Coy.) played the Champion Platoon of the 9th Battn. today at football, but were defeated by 4 Goals to one.	

Army Form C. 2118.

WAR DIARY
of
INTELLIGENCE SUMMARY. 10th Bn. R. Innis. Fus d.
(Erase heading not required.)

Instructions regarding War Diaries and Intelligence Summaries are contained in F. S. Regs. Part II. and the Staff Manual respectively. Title pages will be prepared in manuscript.

Place	Date	Hour	Summary of Events and Information	Remarks and references to Appendices
Bulford Camp	16/3/17		2nd Lieut. H.F.D.O. NOBLE has been reported "Invalided to England" today. The Divisional Baths are Open at our disposal.	
do	17/3/17		2nd Lieut. A. PATTERSON is appointed Intelligence Officer & 2nd Lieut. R.M. BOYLE is appointed LEWIS GUN Officer. 2nd Lieut. C.K. KEVIN invalided to United Kingdom.	
do	18/3/17		The Battalion was relieved by ANZAC's today and took up Billets in the METEREN AREA. Capt. E.H. BARTON arrived today with the Battalion from 12th Res. Battn.	
METEREN	19/3/17		We are stopping in the METEREN AREA today, the Battalion is parading under Company Commanders. 2nd Lieut. R.B. McCONNELL joined today also the other Ranks of a draft. No 20384 Pte. Gill W. proceeded to Base as unfit to carry out the duties of an efficient soldier.	

Army Form C. 2118.

WAR DIARY
INTELLIGENCE SUMMARY.
(Erase heading not required.)

Instructions regarding War Diaries and Intelligence Summaries are contained in F. S. Regs., Part II. and the Staff Manual respectively. Title pages will be prepared in manuscript.

10th B.R. Innis. Fus¹

Place	Date	Hour	Summary of Events and Information	Remarks and references to Appendices
METEREN.	20/3/17		The Battalion left the METEREN AREA today & marched to MORBECQUE, taking over Billets in this town. Distance 10 miles.	
MORBECQUE.	21/3/17		Today we marched to HALLINES, and took over Billets, the Battalion is very fit, and though the march was long, and through a snow storm very few fell 'out'. The route was through ARCQUES, cutting off near ST. OMER. Distance 18 miles.	
HALLINES.	22/3/17		We arrived in ACQUIN today. During the march we have had very bad weather. Snow, hail, and rain almost all the time. Distance 9 miles.	
ACQUIN	23/3/17		The Unit has settled down to work again at the Training. "A" Company practised a Company Attack.	
ACQUIN	24/3/17		a/Capt. R. J. FANNING has been reported as Invalided to United Kingdom sick and is accordingly struck off the Battn. Strength. 2nd/Lieut. R.B.N. SMARTT	

2353 Wt W2544/1454 700,000 5/15 D.D.&L. A.D.S.S./Forms/C. 2118.

WAR DIARY
INTELLIGENCE SUMMARY. 10th Bn. R. Innis. Fus.

Army Form C. 2118.

(Erase heading not required.)

Place	Date	Hour	Summary of Events and Information	Remarks and references to Appendices
ACQUIN.	25/3/17		As stated off the Establishment of the Battalion.	
ACQUIN.	30/3/17		The Battalion is Train Load at Recreation Ground for the Brigade Sports comes off on the 31st instant.	
ACQUIN.	31/3/17		Brigade Sports were held today. Cpl. McClay 'A' Coy. won the Light weight Championship of the Brigade and the Battn. Runners won the Relay Race. No 5 Platoon were the runners up in the Musketry Competition (Inniskilling) having beaten the 9th Battn. (Inniskilling) were defeated by the 11th Battn. (Inniskilling) In the Stretcher Bearer Competition "C" Coy. tied with the 11th Battn. for Second Place. The Platoon Tug of war, No 13 Platoon was beaten by 9th Battn. (Inniskilling) by 2 pulls to one. Cpl. Orr, 'B' Coy was runner up in the Feather Weight Championship.	

Inniskilling. Lt. Coles.

Lt. Coles

CONFIDENTIAL.

W A R D I A R Y

of

10th Battalion Royal Inniskilling Fusiliers,

from 1st April 1917
till 30th   "   1917.

Army Form C. 2118.

WAR DIARY
of 10th R. Innis. Fus.rs
INTELLIGENCE SUMMARY.
(Erase heading not required.)

Instructions regarding War Diaries and Intelligence Summaries are contained in F. S. Regs., Part II. and the Staff Manual respectively. Title pages will be prepared in manuscript.

Place	Date	Hour	Summary of Events and Information	Remarks and references to Appendices
ACQUIN	1/4/17		H.O.R.'s joined the Unit today from 12th Res. Battn. The Battalion strength at present is:— With Battalion 25 Officers 804 Other Ranks In Hospital 1 12 On Leave — 4 On Command 2 70 Making a total of 28 Officers and 890 Other Ranks on the strength of the Unit. Training is still being carried out, the forenoon is used for parading etc. (Including Company and Battalion attacks) and the afternoon with Football etc. Though the weather is extremely unfavourable the Battalion is making good progress.	
ACQUIN	2/4 – 3/4/17		Training continues.	
– do –	4/4/17		At 9.30 a.m. this morning, the Battalion left Acquin for Hallines a distance of 7 miles away.	

Army Form C. 2118.

WAR DIARY
of 10th R. Innis. Fus.
INTELLIGENCE SUMMARY.
(Erase heading not required.)

Instructions regarding War Diaries and Intelligence Summaries are contained in F. S. Regs., Part II. and the Staff Manual respectively. Title pages will be prepared in manuscript.

Place	Date	Hour	Summary of Events and Information	Remarks and references to Appendices
HALLINES.	5/7.		2nd Lt. J. G. Nelson proceeded today to do duty with Commandant ETAPLES, as Officer i/c Reinforcements, and is struck off Establishment of this Battn. Major R. S. Knox proceeded to Aldershot to attend a Commanding Officers Course. The Battalion marched 18 miles today and billeted outside HAZEBROUCK.	
HAZEBROUCK	6/7.		4 Officers joined the Battalion today:- 2nd Lt. W. C. Griffiths, 2nd Lt. J. N. Donnellan, 2nd Lt. R. B. W. Innis and 2nd Lt. A. N. Lindsay. We arrived in Wakefield Huts today having covered 14 miles.	
WAKEFIELD HUTS. near LOCRE.	7/7.		Extract from List No 128 of Appointments dated 24th March. 1917. Temp. Major F. S. N. Macrory D.S.O. (to command Battn) 31st October 1916. vice Major R. S. Knox D.S.O. to be 2nd in Command. The Unit left Wakefield Huts today and proceeded to do Brigade Reserve in the SPANBROEK Sector; Headquarters were in the Curie's House, KEMMEL, C & D Companies were billeted in the Chateau, A Coy at FT. REGINA & EDWARD, and "B" Company at BEEHIVE Dugouts near LINDENHOEK CORNER.	

Army Form C. 2118.

WAR DIARY
of 10th R. Innis. Fus.
INTELLIGENCE SUMMARY.
(Erase heading not required.)

Place	Date	Hour	Summary of Events and Information	Remarks and references to Appendices
SPANBROEK SECTOR.	8th/14 – 13th/17		Working Parties. On the 9th a draft of 1st R. Innis. Fus. joined the Battalion.	
-do-	14th/17		We relieved the 11th R. Innis. Fus. today in the trenches, relief began after dark as most of the roads are under the enemy's observation. Headquarters at Fort Victoria, "C" & "D" Coys. in the Front Line & "A" & "B" doing Reserves. The enemy is very quiet, Artillery etc. very quiet.	
-do-	15th/17 – 17th/17		"C" & "D" Coys. were relieved in the Front Line by "A" & "B" Coys.	
-do-	17th/17			
-do-	18th/17		Enemy's Artillery etc. very quiet in the Battalion Sector, towards nightfall (7 pm) a German was seen coming across "No Man's Land" running from one shell hole to another, apparently giving himself up as a prisoner. Unluckily a Trench Mortar N.C.O. fired at him and seemingly wounded him, so he began to run back to his own wire again. Before he reached his own wire, some of the Battalion fired and he fell. At 9.30 pm. a patrol went out to find him, but	

Army Form C. 2118.

WAR DIARY
of 10th Ry. Innis. Fus.
INTELLIGENCE SUMMARY.

(Erase heading not required.)

Place	Date	Hour	Summary of Events and Information	Remarks and references to Appendices
HAZEBROUCK SECTOR	19/7		he had been taken in. A draft of 3 ORs joined today.	
			Very quiet during the day. A patrol of was sent out at 9.0 p.m. to throw bottles with messages inside (asking the Germans over) into the line – it was thought that the German who had been fired upon, was only a forerunner, and others were waiting to see if he landed all right.	
do.	20/7		About 6 p.m. a Boche came over to our lines and surrendered himself to A Coy. having been interrogated by an Interpreter, he said there were 8 others who would come across if he could possibly signal them. Accordingly at 8 p.m. the prisoner went across "no man's land" to fetch his comrades, but he was forced to come back again, having lost his way. He tried once more to get across, but the Germans holding the line fired on him and he came back again unsuccessful. Later he was handed over to Brigade Headquarters. A draft of 25 ORs joined today. The Battalion withdrew into Brigade.	

Army Form C. 2118.

WAR DIARY
of 10th R. Innis. Fus.
INTELLIGENCE SUMMARY.

(Erase heading not required.)

Place	Date	Hour	Summary of Events and Information	Remarks and references to Appendices
	20th/7		Reserve, relief began at 8 p.m. Headquarters being in Kemmel Chateau, "A" & "B" in Chateau, "C" in Forts Regina & Edward and "D" Coy at BEEHIVE Dugouts (See map attached) Enemy's aircraft very busy.	
KEMMEL	21st/7		Working parties. 2nd Lt. E. H. Lambert joined the Battalion today.	
- do -	22nd/7 - 24th/7		Enemy's aircraft very active. Working Parties.	
- do -	25th/7		Enemy's artillery active all night, a great number of H. 2. Howitzer shells exploded in the vicinity of the CHATEAU, wounding 1 man, otherwise no damage was done. It is thought that he was searching for Batteries lying near the village. 3 ORs joined Battn. on draft. Working Parties are cancelled for tonight.	
- do -	26th/7		The Battalion relieved the 11th R. Innis. Fus. in the Right Subsector today. Details (Lewis Gunners, Signallers etc) relieved in the afternoon, others at 8 p.m.	

Army Form C. 2118.

WAR DIARY of 10th R. Innis. Fus.
INTELLIGENCE SUMMARY.
(Erase heading not required.)

Instructions regarding War Diaries and Intelligence Summaries are contained in F.S. Regs., Part II and the Staff Manual respectively. Title pages will be prepared in manuscript.

Place	Date	Hour	Summary of Events and Information	Remarks and references to Appendices
SPANBROEK SECTOR.	27th/17		"A" Coy. proceeded to the Right Front with Headquarters of Coy. at BATTLE HQ; "B" to the left Front with Headquarters at Ulster Road; "C" Coy. to Right Support with Headquarters at COOKER FARM; and "D" Coy. to Left Reserve with Headquarters at S.P.4. Battalion Headquarters took over NEWPORT DUGOUTS (see map attached)	
			Aeroplanes (British) very busy. With the exception of some H.E. Shells, which fell in the vicinity of R.E. FARM, and a few Minenwerfers in Ulster Road, the day was fairly quiet. At about 10pm, the German Trench Mortars sent over some bombs, our Artillery & Trench Mortars retaliated effectively. Our casualties were 1 wounded and 1 Shell Shocked.	
- do -	28th/17		Our Artillery were very busy all day. The enemy retaliated on KEMMEL village. At 5pm. our Trench Mortars were very busy, the bombardment lasted one hour, enemy retaliated with Trench Mortars and H.E. Shells. Our Casualties were 1 killed & 1 wounded.	

Army Form C. 2118.

WAR DIARY
of 10th Ry. Susic. Iust.
INTELLIGENCE SUMMARY.
(Erase heading not required.)

Instructions regarding War Diaries and Intelligence Summaries are contained in F. S. Regs., Part II. and the Staff Manual respectively. Title pages will be prepared in manuscript.

Place	Date	Hour	Summary of Events and Information	Remarks and references to Appendices
SPANBROEK SECTOR.	29/4/17.		Our Aircraft very busy all day, at about 5pm. about 7 of our planes went across enemy's lines. they were shelled very heavily. An enemy plane came over our lines about one hour afterwards, but was turned by our Anti-Aircraft Guns. Our artillery were very active all day, enemy retaliated on KEMMEL Village. Shrapnel was seen bursting over Messines at the same time. Inter Company relief took place today relief was complete by 10pm.	
-do-	30/4/17.		At 4.10 a.m. this morning, our Artillery & Trench mortars bombarded enemy's lines on the extreme right of our Sub. Sector. The bombardment lasted about one hour. Enemy put over a few Minenwerfers into the line occupied by "C" Coy. The artillery have been very busy all forenoon, they are shelling very far behind Enemy's line, to the left of Messines. About a dozen WHIZZ-BANGS lit behind COOKER FARM at 9.30 a.m. The afternoon was fairly quiet. British Aeroplanes still active. Enemy shelled Kemmel village very heavily during the afternoon with H.E shells & heavy Shrapnel. Our artillery retaliated and became more active as darkness fell. Enemy retaliated at about 4.30pm. on KINGSWAY wounding 7men.	

2353 Wt. W2541/1454 700,000 5/15 D.D.&L. A.D.S.S./Forms/C. 2118.

Army Form C. 2118.

WAR DIARY
of 10th Ry. Innis. Fus.
INTELLIGENCE SUMMARY.
(Erase heading not required.)

Place	Date	Hour	Summary of Events and Information	Remarks and references to Appendices
	30th		The Battalion Strength is as follows :—	
			With Battalion 26 Officers 496 Other Ranks	
			Hospital 3"	
			Leave 1 5	
			On Command 5 157	
			Total 31 922	
			On the 28th Major E.W. Crawford 9th Ry. Innis. Fusrs. joined the Battn. acting as 2nd in Command during the absence of Major R.S. Knox. During the month 1 Off. & 7 ORs. went on leave to U.K. 2nd Lt. H.C. Beale to England 9.4.17 is struck off the Battn. Strength from 27/17. 2nd Lt. H.N. Lindsay was appointed Signalling Officer; 2nd Lt. A. Patterson Intelligence Officer; 2nd Lt. R.M. Boyle Lewis Gun Officer and 2nd Lt. S.M.H. Mark Bombing Officer and Works Officer. On the 30th 2nd Lt. H. Drummond, 2nd Lt. A. Bogle, 2nd Lt. A.G. Richardson and 2nd Lt. J.A. Caskey joined the Battn. from 12th Res. Battn. 2 ORs. also joined.	Murray Lt. Colonel. Comdg 10th R. Innis. Fus.

CONFIDENTIAL.

WAR DIARY

OF

10TH. BATTALION ROYAL INNISKILLING FUSILIERS.

FROM 1ST. MAY, 1917.

TILL 31ST. MAY, 1917.

WAR DIARY of 19th R. Innis. Fus.
INTELLIGENCE SUMMARY

Army Form C. 2118.

(Erase heading not required.)

Place	Date	Hour	Summary of Events and Information	Remarks and references to Appendices
SPANBROEK SECTOR. (Brigade Right Sector)	1/5/17		Enemy's artillery very active all day, he shelled KINGSWAY TRENCH near BEEHIVES, (N.34.b.), also KEMMEL Village and the Batteries behind NEWPORT DUGOUTS (N.34.b.) with H.E. Shells, shrapnel and WHIZZ-BANGS. There were no casualties in the Battalion. About 1 p.m. an observation Balloon was seen far behind and to the left of MESSINES. One of our Aviators tried to bring it down, but was shelled very heavily and had to withdraw, meanwhile the Balloon was taken down and raised again when the air was clear of our machines. Our aeroplanes were very busy all day, sometimes 5 and 6 machines were far over the Boche lines, some were very heavily shelled, but none were hit. British Artillery have given the enemy no peace whatever, shrapnel was continually seen bursting over the centre of MESSINES.	
	2/5/17		The wind is in Enemy's favour today. The enemy has shelled KEMMEL & KINGSWAY (in the neighbourhood of BEEHIVES) all forenoon with intervals. Towards mid-day many shelled FRENCHMANS FARM, (S.E. of NEWPORT DUGOUTS) with Gas Shells. This farm was a Machine Gun Post, the Gunners stopping in a large dugout. All the Gunners were gassed or wounded. Two men of "A" Coy, went round immediately	

Army Form C. 2118.

WAR DIARY
of
INTELLIGENCE SUMMARY.
(Erase heading not required.)

10th R. Innis. Fus.

Place	Date	Hour	Summary of Events and Information	Remarks and references to Appendices
SPANBROEK SECTOR.	2/5/17		to the Gunners aid, and shewed great gallantry in rescuing the Lew. Crew. Three men were No. 15546 Pte. Lennon J. (who has repeatedly shewn a good example in devotion to duty) and No. 40643 Pte. Galway R.I. An enemy plane came over our lines in the afternoon, but was forced to return by our Anti-aircraft Guns. We were relieved today by the 14th R.I. Rifles, relief began at 8 p.m. The Battalion retired into Brigade Reserve at KEMMEL village relieving the 11th R. Innis. Fus. "A" Coy at FORT REGINA (N.28.a.) and FORT EDWARD (N.34.b.) and "B" Coy at KEMMEL BEEHIVES (N.29.a.); "C" & "D" Coys at KEMMEL CHATEAU and Battalion Headquarters at CURE'S HOUSE. During relief the Lew Alarm sounded on left, but as no signs of gas were seen or felt it must have been gas shells or a false alarm. We had two casualties today, a man of "C" Coy was wounded by shrapnel from a trench mortar and one of "D" Coy by shrapnel also from a trench mortar, the latter however remained with Battalion, after being inoculated. Relief was complete at 11 p.m.	
KEMMEL	3/5/17 5/5/17		Working Parties.	

2353 Wt. W2344/1454 700,000 5/15 L.D.&L. A.D.S.S./Forms/C. 2118.

Army Form C. 2118.

WAR DIARY
of
INTELLIGENCE SUMMARY.
(Erase heading not required.)

10th R. Innis. Fus.

Instructions regarding War Diaries and Intelligence Summaries are contained in F. S. Regs. Part II. and the Staff Manual respectively. Title pages will be prepared in manuscript.

Place	Date	Hour	Summary of Events and Information	Remarks and references to Appendices
KEMMEL.	6/5/17		Working Parties as usual. The Enemy shelled KEMMEL VILLAGE & especially the Chateau during the night. British artillery replied effectively. Aircraft of both sides were active during the day.	
	7/5/17		Working Parties. Enemy again shelled KEMMEL & surroundings, our artillery are always active.	
SPANBROEK SECTOR	8/5/17		We relieved the 11th R. Innis. Fusiliers today in the Right Sector of Brigade. "C" & "D" Companies took over the Front Line, the other Companies the Support line. "A" Coy. supporting "C" & "D" Cos. supporting "D". Relief was complete at 10 p.m. Headquarters were situated at FORT VICTORIA (N. 28. C.) Enemy shelled the communication trenches at 10.30 p.m. with shrapnel, wounding 11 men, one remaining with Unit. The 16th Division are on our left and the 9th Inniskillings on our right.	
	9/5/17		Enemy was quiet all day, our artillery are still active; Our Aircraft extremely busy. 14 ORs. joined today from Base Depot. No 39497 Pte. McFarland J.J. died of wounds received yesterday. Lieut. G. D. TAYLOR proceeded to ETAPLES as Draft conducting Officer. (Auth. 36th Divi. C/118 of 9.5.17)	

Army Form C. 2118.

WAR DIARY
of
INTELLIGENCE SUMMARY.
(Erase heading not required.)

10th R. Innis: Fus. C

Instructions regarding War Diaries and Intelligence Summaries are contained in F. S. Regs., Part II. and the Staff Manual respectively. Title pages will be prepared in manuscript.

Place	Date	Hour	Summary of Events and Information	Remarks and references to Appendices
SPANBROEK SECTOR	10/5/17 & 11/5/17		Very Quiet. "A" & "B" Coys relieved "C" & "D" in the Front Line today, the latter Companies retired into Support.	
	12/5/17		About mid-day our planes owing to mist had to descend, while they were away an Enemy machine came across and leisurely crossed over KEMMEL flying in the direction of ARMENTIERES at about an altitude of 500 feet. Our Lewis Gun team at FORT VICTORIA fired on it, but every to the darkness caused by rain no anti-aircraft guns opened fire, so the aviator must have observed a good deal. 2nd Lieut. W.C. Griffiths proceeded today to the 2nd Army Central School at WISQUES.	
	13/5/17		Enemy shelled KEMMEL very heavily with H.E. Shells, otherwise very quiet.	
WAKEFIELD HUTS	14/5/17		The Battalion was relieved by the 11th Rifle Brigade in the Front Line today. After relief the Battalion retired into Divisional Reserve. "A" Coy to N.19.a. 9.4. "B" Coy to N.25.C. with "C" Coys and "D" Coys to M.24 Central. Battalion Headquarters proceeded to WAKEFIELD HUTS. (M.29.C) (7 ORS 10/4 joined the 7th)	
	15/5/17		Working Parties	

Army Form C. 2118.

WAR DIARY
of
INTELLIGENCE SUMMARY. 10th R. Innis. Fus.

(Erase heading not required.)

Instructions regarding War Diaries and Intelligence Summaries are contained in F.S. Regs., Part II. and the Staff Manual respectively. Title pages will be prepared in manuscript.

Place	Date	Hour	Summary of Events and Information	Remarks and references to Appendices
WAKEFIELD	16/5/17.		Working Parties. 12 ORs Draft joined Battn. from Base Depot.	
HUTS.	17/5/17 & 20/5/17		Working Parties.	
	21/5/17.		Working Parties. 18 ORs. joined Battalion from Base Depot.	
	22/5/17.		"	
	23/5/17.		" Lieut. L.C. Griffiths returned from Courts at 2nd Army School.	
	24/5/17		" 7 ORs. Draft joined Bay.	
	25/5/17		" 2nd Lieut. J. Bennett proceeded to a Stokes Mortar Courts.	
	26 & 27/5/17		"	
	28/5/17.		At 2.40 a.m. the enemy bombarded the DRANOUTRE – LOCRE Road, and the Appent camps on it with heavy Shrapnel & H.E. Shells for about one hour. One man of the Battn. attacked temporarily to the 150th Coy. R.E. was wounded	

WAR DIARY
of
INTELLIGENCE SUMMARY.
(Erase heading not required.)

Army Form C. 2118.

10th R. Innis. Fus.

Place	Date	Hour	Summary of Events and Information	Remarks and references to Appendices
WAKEFIELD HUTS	28/5/17		Working Parties. 2nd Lieut. A. J. Stair who proceeded on leave 11th, marked "Medical Board & report & return" has been struck off the strength of this Unit. (Auth. 2nd Army No A/729 of 21.5.17). 2nd Lieut Chambers proceeded to 2nd Army Central School to undergo a Grenade Course. Signalling McClatchi	
	29/5/17		Very early this morning the enemy bombarded WAKEFIELD HUTS, the bombardment began with WHIZZ-BANGS Shrapnel & H.E.s were also thrown. The transport men were forced to take the Animals to a place of safety on the LOCRE - BAILLEUL Road. The DRANOUTRE - LOCRE Road was very heavily shelled with Shrapnel & HEs. Also a Artillery around line behind WAKEFIELD HUTS. Bombardment lasted one hour. Enemy began again to bombard with WHIZZ-BANGS at 10.30 a.m. The first shell exploded in the field in front of the Transport lines, all kinds of shells were thrown in the vicinity of WAKEFIELD forcing most of the Troops there to leave the Camp & there is a wood behind. The bombardments are most likely due to information given by a German aviator who flew over this place about noon 26/5.	
	30/5/17		Enemy again bombarded at 1 a.m., the bombardment was similar to last nights.	

Army Form C. 2118.

WAR DIARY
of
INTELLIGENCE SUMMARY.
(Erase heading not required.) 10th A. Innis: ???

Instructions regarding War Diaries and Intelligence Summaries are contained in F. S. Regs., Part II. and the Staff Manual respectively. Title pages will be prepared in manuscript.

Place	Date	Hour	Summary of Events and Information	Remarks and references to Appendices
WAKEFIELD	30/5/17		We had one Casualty, a man attacked to the 109th Light Trench Mortar Battery. Working Parties are carried on as usual day and night.	
HUTS.	31/5/17		Another Straffe this morning, a few shells exploded near WAKEFIELD, the bombardment was similar to the preceding ones. No casualties.	
			The following Officers joined on dates shewn against their names:—	
			2nd Lieut J. M. Bennett. 3. 5. 17.	
			" K. C. McCatchie "	
			" J Mitchell "	
			" W. A. Knox "	
			" R. G. Neill 6. 5. 17. (This Officer has been with Battn. before)	
			" L. S. May. 6. 5. 17.	
			" P. S. McBride 13. 5. 17.	

2353 Wt. W2344/1454 700,000 5/15 D. D. & L. A.D.S.S./Forms/C. 2118.

Army Form C. 2118.

WAR DIARY
of
INTELLIGENCE SUMMARY.

(Erase heading not required.)

10th R. Innis. Fus.

Place	Date	Hour	Summary of Events and Information	Remarks and references to Appendices
			Battalion Strength. 1st May 1914.	
			O.s W.Os ORs 31.5.17.	
			With Battalion 29 6 720 O.s W.Os ORs.	
			Hospital 31 32 4 799	
			Leave 1 4 2 12	
			On Command etc. 5 157 2 20	
			6 135	
			Total 35 6 912. 40 6 966.	
			2 Officers and 76 Other Ranks proceeded on Leave to U.K. during month.	
			Summary. Lieut. Colonel,	
			Commdg. 10th (S) Batn. R. Innis. Fus.	

WAR DIARY FOR MONTH OF JUNE 1917.

10TH. ROYAL INNISKILLING FUSILIERS.

Ref. Map. 28. S.W. WYTSCHAETE 1a. 1b. 10,000.
Army Form C. 2118.

WAR DIARY
of
INTELLIGENCE SUMMARY.
(Erase heading not required.)

10th R. Inns. Fus.

Place	Date	Hour	Summary of Events and Information	Remarks and references to Appendices
WAKEFIELD HUTS.	1/7		The Battalion is employed with R.E.'s v R.F.A., digging Assembly Trenches, constructing advanced Gun Pits, and as carrying parties. At 6 p.m. this evening Headquarters (less Q.M. Store) and Regtl. Transport moved to BERTHEN AREA (M.13.D.D.) H.Q. marched in two parties at 200 yds. interval, through MONT NOIR. They were accommodated in Tents and Bivouacs, the weather conditions are extremely favourable. 7 O.R.s. proceeded to U.K. on leave; 4 O.R.s. rejoined Battalion from 171st Tunnelling Company. R.E.	
BERTHEN AREA.	2/7		The Companies are still employed on Working Parties. 50 O.R.s. remaining with 171st Tunn. Coy. R.E. rejoined to day.	
-do-	3/7		Battalion. Headquarters attended a Brigade Service conducted by C. of E. Rev. Shapland at M.13.6.6.1. Companies are still employed with Working Parties. 9 # O.R.s. have been attached to C.R.E. until further orders. 2nd Lt. Mitchell & 4 O.R.s proceeded to LA LEVRETTE on Bombing Course.	
-do-	4/7		Companies finished work with R.E.'s v R.F.A. and rejoined Headquarters at 8½ p.m. The Brigade is together now in one Camp. 4 O.R.'s proceeded to Army Rest Camp; 5 O.R.s Joined Draft joined from Base.	

WAR DIARY of INTELLIGENCE SUMMARY.

10th Bn. Rl. Innis. Fus.

(Erase heading not required.)

Army Form C. 2118.

Place	Date	Hour	Summary of Events and Information	Remarks and references to Appendices
BERTHEN AREA	5/7		At 5 p.m. the Battalion proceed to practice attack, returning to Camp at 10.30 a.m. 5 ORs. proceeded on Leave to U.K.	
-do-	6/7		The Battalion marched to WAKEFIELD HUTS (M.29.c.8.1.) by Platoons at 200 yds. interval. Camp was struck at 8 a.m.; tents & Bivouacs were stacked and and left in charge of guard to be later over by Divisional supernumerary. When nearing our destination enemy shelled the road behind WAKEFIELD WOOD, no damage was done and shelling soon ceased. Dispositions:– H.Q. in HUTS, Companies in WOOD (M.29.c.) The afternoon was spent in resting. During the evening Bombs, ammunition, solidified alcohol, chocolate etc. were issued, and fighting kit was inspected by Platoon Commanded Haversacks and greatcoats (which came from BERTHEN AREA in bundles of ten) were taken over by Quarter Master. Battalion Headquarters followed by Platoons at 200 yds interval left for the assembly trenches at 10 p.m. Dispositions:– H.Q. at N.29.c.7.9. Q.M. Stores & Transport Lines, Officers & ORs detailed to remain stopped at WAKEFIELD HUTS (M.29.c.8.1.) Enemy shelled all round KEMMEL HILL with heavy shrapnel, while Battn. was marching up.	

2353 Wt. W2544/1454 700,000 5/15 D.D.&L. A.D.S.S./Forms/C. 2118.

WAR DIARY
of
INTELLIGENCE SUMMARY. 10th Cy. Innis. Fus.

(Erase heading not required.)

Army Form C. 2118.

Place	Date	Hour	Summary of Events and Information	Remarks and references to Appendices
SPANBROEK SECTOR.	7/6/17		See attached Operation Orders & Amendments, MAP and Narrative of Battle, needless to say the Battalion took all its objectives. Held them. Zero time was 3.10 a.m.	
Do -	8/6/17		At 3 a.m. was withdrawn into Support - Reserve Headquarters at REGENT STREET DUGOUTS (M.29.c.7.) The Companies bivouaced at FORT REGINA, during the afternoon details left behind at WAKEFIELD HUTS joined the Battalion. At 6 p.m. a Salvage Party of under one Officer with 10 Pack Mules searched the ground fought over on preceding day, for useful material, these were dumped. At 7 p.m. our artillery became very active in retaliation for enemy fire, shortly afterwards orders was given to "Stand to". The enemy counter attacked our new position, but supports were not called for, so the Battn. "Stand Down" and the night passed off quietly.	
WAKEFIELD HUTS.	9/6/17		At 10 a.m. the Battalion marched back to WAKEFIELD HUTS, Companies bivouac in wood (M.29.C.) Our casualties were 4 OR's Killed, 1 Died of wounds, 50 wounded on 7th Inst. 2nd Lt. H. Richardson was wounded. OR's proceeded to U.K. on leave.	

Army Form C. 2118.

WAR DIARY
of
INTELLIGENCE SUMMARY. 10th Bn. Innis. Fus.

(Erase heading not required.)

Instructions regarding War Diaries and Intelligence Summaries are contained in F. S. Regs., Part II and the Staff Manual respectively. Title pages will be prepared in manuscript.

Place	Date	Hour	Summary of Events and Information	Remarks and references to Appendices
WAKEFIELD HUTS.	10/6/17		All Companies paraded for work on WYTSCHAETE - WULVERGHEM Road, Rendezvous SHELL FARM (N.36.c.3.8) at 7 a.m. They returned to WAKEFIELD WOOD at 5 p.m. One man was died. 1600 Pte. S.J. Simpson & 20036 Pte. G. McGuire passed the necessary test as 1st Class Signallers.	
- do -	11/6/17		Companies engaged on Road making again. Bivouacs were provided at FORT VICTORIA (written) they were withdrawn on completion of days work.	
- do -	12/6/17		Working Parties as yesterday, on completion of days work. Coys were withdrawn to WAKEFIELD WOOD, being relieved by 9th R. Innis. Fus.	
MONT NOIR.	13/6/17		At 1.15 p.m. the Battalion marched on MONT NOIR, though DRANOUTRE. Order of march :- H.Q. D, C, B & A Coy. On line of march the Battn. was inspected by the Corps Commander. The New Camp consisting of tents was reached at about 7 p.m. (M.20.D.75) Qm. Store & Transport Lines (M.20.D.75.50)	

Army Form C. 2118.

WAR DIARY
of
INTELLIGENCE SUMMARY. 10th Ry. Innis. Fus.

(Erase heading not required.)

Instructions regarding War Diaries and Intelligence Summaries are contained in F.S. Regs., Part II. and the Staff Manual respectively. Title pages will be prepared in manuscript.

Place	Date	Hour	Summary of Events and Information	Remarks and references to Appendices
MONT NOIR	14/6/17		The Battalion paraded at 10 a.m.; they were addressed by Brig. Genl. Ricardo and Lieut Colonel Macrory, who congratulated the Battn. on the splendid work done by all ranks on the 7th inst. Brig. Genl. Ricardo has the Corps Commanders congratulations to the "Derrys". During the absence of Major E.W. Crayford, 2nd in command (who took over duties in Brigade Office) Capt. E.H. Barton took over duties, Maj. S.H.A. Watt took over O.C. B. Coy. vice Capt. E.H. Barton. 2nd Lt. Capt. A.F. Cook who has been Acting Brigade Transport Officer since 5th inst rejoined the Battn. and took over O.C. H Coy. from 2nd Lt. J. McMeekan 2nd Lt. T.W. Boyce. At 5 O.C.s. proceeded on leave to U.K.	
-do-	15/6/17		Companies training under Coy. Commanders. 15670 Sgt. L. Kirby took over C.S.M's duties of H. Coy. vice C.S.M. Irwin. R.S. wounded 7/6	
-do-	16/6/17		In the evening Companies under Coy. arrangements marched to FORT VICTORIA to relieve 9th R. Innis. Fus. engaged on work on WYTSCHAETE – WULVERGHEM Road. Draft of 10 O.Rs. joined Battn. today	

Army Form C. 2118.

WAR DIARY
INTELLIGENCE SUMMARY.
(Erase heading not required.)

10th Bn. Suss. Regt.

Instructions regarding War Diaries and Intelligence Summaries are contained in F.S. Regs., Part II. and the Staff Manual respectively. Title pages will be prepared in manuscript.

Place	Date	Hour	Summary of Events and Information	Remarks and references to Appendices
MONT NOIR.	17/6/17		Companies engaged on Working Parties. Draft of 30 O.R.s joined today.	
WESTON CAMP near LOCRE.	18/6/17		At 6.30 p.m. Batt. H.Q. & Details marched to WESTON CAMP (M. 17. a. 7. 8.) being joined by Coys. from FT. VICTORIA at about 10 p.m.	
SPANBROEK SECTOR.	19/6/17		At 6 p.m. Battalion moved off by platoons at 200 yds. interval to relieve the 10th Warwicks (57th Bgde. 19th Division) in Support at O.15.A.7.T, O.14.A. & O.9.A. Batt. Headquarters at O.14.A.45.43. Fauquart Lines at O.M. Stores at N.10.A.3.5. As there were no shelters here, Battalion had to commence & construct temporary dugouts. One man "C" Coy was wounded.	
do.	20/6/17		The enemy shelled all round, mostly at Artillery positions all day. A few H.E. shells dropped at "B" Coys dugouts. 4 men were wounded. On 1570th Pte. S. Loakes afterwards Died from effects of wounds. Coys were also doing Working Parties.	
do.	21/6/17		The enemy shelled all round today. Enemy aircraft extremely busy.	

Army Form C. 2118.

WAR DIARY
of
INTELLIGENCE SUMMARY.
(Erase heading not required.)

10th Ry. Snrs. Fus.

Instructions regarding War Diaries and Intelligence Summaries are contained in F.S. Regs., Part II. and the Staff Manual respectively. Title pages will be prepared in manuscript.

Place	Date	Hour	Summary of Events and Information	Remarks and references to Appendices
SPANBROEK SECTOR	21/6/17		30 O.Rs. Draft joined today from Base Depot.	
	22/6/17		Enemy's aircraft and artillery extremely busy, to has been bombarding all over with heavy H.E. & Shrapnel Shells. Many shells exploded in the vicinity of Boys & H.Qrs. 16082 Pte. Walter J. was killed by H.E. Shell. 30 O.Rs. Draft joined today.	
-do-	24/6/17		Shelling still continued also aerial activity. The enemy's planes very frequently come over our lines, firing his machine guns etc. They have also been extremely successful in bringing down some of our Kite-Balloons. 23248 Pte. J. Wilson was killed by H.E. Shell today, also 7 O.Rs. wounded by same shell.	
-do-	25/6/17		Enemy's shelling has somewhat increased today, at all times our guns retaliate effectively. His planes are more active, and seem to never mind our Arca guns. Luckily nobody was hit today. The Battalion relieved the 11th R. Innis. Fus. in the front line tonight. There was very heavy rain during the relief.	

Army Form C. 2118.

WAR DIARY
of
INTELLIGENCE SUMMARY.

(Erase heading not required.)

19th Rfl. Innis. Fus.

Instructions regarding War Diaries and Intelligence Summaries are contained in F.S. Regs., Part II. and the Staff Manual respectively. Title pages will be prepared in manuscript.

Place	Date	Hour	Summary of Events and Information	Remarks and references to Appendices
SPANBROEK MOLEN	26/7		Enemy still active. No. 15317 Pte. T. Finlay & 1939 Pte. J. Faik killed today. 5 ORs wounded by H.E. shell. An enemy airman flew very low over our lines and circled round and returned to his own lines. Our aircraft guns killed him and two or three machine guns were turned on him. The enemy aircraft on this front has a red tinge round the plane, and it is rumoured that they are manned by the best airmen in Germany.	
Do	27/7		Enemy still active. An enemy aviator came across and set a Balloon on fire. Artillery behind our Q.M. Stores, both occupants of Balloon escaped by para chute. 5 ORs. went on leave on 22nd; L. Moon & 5 ORs on 18th & Lieut on leave Maj. J.W. Davidson & 3 ORs went to MOULLE TEUSE Rest Camp on 18/7/7. 3 ORs wounded by Lyme 27/7.	
Do	28/7		At 10.45 p.m. a fighting patrol consisting of two officers and 20 ORs left our line (O.16.a.99.80) for the purpose of gaining information and identification of the forces opposing us. An enemy patrol was seen but had gone off before our men arrived. Our patrol proceeded 500 yds. but no signs of enemy was to be seen.	

Army Form C. 2118.

WAR DIARY
INTELLIGENCE SUMMARY.
(Erase heading not required.)

10th Regt. Inns. Fus.

Instructions regarding War Diaries and Intelligence Summaries are contained in F.S. Regs., Part II. and the Staff Manual respectively. Title pages will be prepared in manuscript.

Place	Date	Hour	Summary of Events and Information	Remarks and references to Appendices
SCHARPEN-BERG	29/7		Our Casualties to-day were one wounded. The Battalion was relieved in the Front Line tonight by the 4th Middlesex Regt. relief began at 12.0 p.m. and completed at 4.30 a.m. 30/7. The Transport Lines & Q.M. Stores were relieved during the day & proceeded to DE ZON Camp (near Locre) Whither the Battalion also came after relief, relieving the 8th Lincolnshire Regt. 2nd/Lt. R.J. Tanning joined the Battn. to-day. 1st/Lt. Botts transferred to-day. One man was wounded to-day.	
DE ZON CAMP, near LOCRE				
Do	30/7		The Battalion stopped all day at DE ZON Camp, recuperating after a strenuous time in the line. It is interesting to note that the enemy did not know our forward position in the line, and he shelled both in front & rear of our front line, also at artillery positions far behind all the time the Battn. was in support in the trenches. Enemy is using guns of hy. calibre, seldom does one hear a Field piece. During our tour little or no machine gun fire was heard.	

2353 Wt W3344/1454 700,000 5/15 D. D. & L. A.D.S.S./Forms/C. 2118.

WAR DIARY
INTELLIGENCE SUMMARY
(Erase heading not required.)

10th Regl. Innis. Fust.

Army Form C. 2118.

Battalion Strength Compared:—

	1st June 1917.			30th June 1917.		
	Off	5 WOs	794 ORs	Off	5 WOs	779 ORs
With Battalion	32	–	132	30	–	68
On Command	6	1	22	5	–	19
On Leave	–	*	1	1	–	–
In Hospital	2	–	10	3	–	28
Total	40	6	961	39	5	894

During the month Hon. Lieut. & Hon. Other Ranks proceeded to U.K. on Leave.
Captain J. S. Paton C.F. attached to this Unit was awarded the Military Cross.
Lieut. Col. McCrory proceeded on Leave to United Kingdom 30/6/17.
* R.S.M. J. Galbraith proceeded on Leave and was admitted to Hospital in Belfast.
Captain A. E. Boot proceeded on Leave to U.K. 20/6/17.

E. H. Borton Capt
O C 10th R Innis Fus

10TH ROYAL INNISKILLING FUSILIERS.

WAR DIARY

for

MONTH of JULY, 1917.

Army Form C. 2118.

WAR DIARY
of
INTELLIGENCE SUMMARY.

10th R. Innis. Fus.

(Erase heading not required.)

Instructions regarding War Diaries and Intelligence Summaries are contained in F.S. Regs., Part II. and the Staff Manual respectively. Title pages will be prepared in manuscript.

Place	Date	Hour	Summary of Events and Information	Remarks and references to Appendices
DE ZON Camp near LOCRE.	1/7/17		Reference Map. 27. S.E. 1/20,000. 1 Other Rank (Transport) proceeded to ST. OMER today on a Veterinary Course. The Battalion marched to the STRAZEELE area this morning at 8am. They moved by LOCRE - MONT NOIR - METEREN to ROUGE CROIX (W. 10. c. 00. 00. CAESTRE.) The men's packs were carried by the Regimental Transport, who had to complete the 2nd journey. During the march, near METEREN 8 r.c. Coys. broke off and proceeded to c. 20. a. 1. 9 for Baths, afterwards rejoining the Battn. at CAESTRE. This is the anniversary of the Ulster Division's charge at THIEPVAL, SOMME.	
CAESTRE.	2/7/17		6 O.R's joined Battalion from 36th (Ulster) Division Base Depot: 12 OR's serving with the 109th L.I.M. Battery have been transferred under Authority G.R.O. 2394. Major R.S. Knox who has been on a C.O.'s Course at ALDERSHOT returned today, & took over duties from Capt. E.H. Baxton who had been acting Commanding Officer. Extract:- Temp. 2/Lt. (T/Lt.) J.S. Allen to be acting Captain whilst commanding 109th L.I.M. Battery.16/1.7. No. 10372 Sgt Hamilton R. B. Coy appointed a/C.S.M. as from 28/6/17 vice C.S.M Tulbert B.Coys. to U.K. Inspections were carried out today by Co. & Company Commanders. Bdy some Drills.	

Army Form C. 2118.

WAR DIARY
of
10th R. Innis. Fus.
INTELLIGENCE SUMMARY.

(Erase heading not required.)

Instructions regarding War Diaries and Intelligence Summaries are contained in F. S. Regs., Part II. and the Staff Manual respectively. Title pages will be prepared in manuscript.

Place	Date	Hour	Summary of Events and Information	Remarks and references to Appendices
CAESTRE.	3/7/17		At 8am. this morning the Battalion was inspected by Brig. General Ricardo. Duties as usual were carried out during the forenoon.	
- do -	4/7/17		2nd Lieut. L.W. Davidson & 4 ORs. rejoined from Army Rest Camp. Captain C.N.K. Strange & Capt. S.E. Peelan with 5 ORs. proceeded to U.K. on Leave. Parades as usual in the forenoon.	
- do -	5/7/17		The Battalion left CAESTRE and marched to the HONDEGHEM ( ) Area and Bivouaced in Farms for the night. Distance covered about 5 miles.	
HONDEGHEM AREA.	6/7/17		2nd Lieut. O.H. Peelan to U.K. 20/6/17, granted 2 weeks sick leave by Medical Board, to attend Battn. Strength. The Battn. marched to ARQUES AREA to-day. the Camp was beside a lake and nothing was permitted. Distance covered today was about 8 miles.	
ARQUES.	7/7/17		4 ORs. to transferred to this Unit from 9th Battn. R. Innis. Fus.	

Army Form C. 2118.

WAR DIARY
of
INTELLIGENCE SUMMARY.   10th R. Innis. Fust.

(Erase heading not required.)

Instructions regarding War Diaries and Intelligence Summaries are contained in F. S. Regs., Part II. and the Staff Manual respectively. Title pages will be prepared in manuscript.

Place	Date	Hour	Summary of Events and Information	Remarks and references to Appendices
			Reference map. CALAIS. 13/100,000.	
	7/7/17		The Battn. marched to HAUT LOQUIN today. Distance covered was about 22 miles. The Battalion left Arques at 2.30 a.m. and arrived about 12 noon and were accommodated in farms etc.	
HAUT LOQUIN.	8/7/17		2nd Lt. Chambers is appointed Battn. Bombing Officer. Rewards:- The IXth Corps Commander under authority delegated by H.M. the King has awarded the Military Medal to the following N.C.O.s & men. 16012 Pte. Sinclair A.; 16025 Sgt. Spiers J.; 15631 L.Cpl. Lineaghan J.; 15909 Cpl. Nicholl J.S.; 19095 L.Cpl. Hassan M. 1 Officer & 6 O.Rs. proceeded to U.K. on Leave.	
-do-	9/7/17		26 O.Rs. joined from Base Depot. 4 O.Rs. exchanged with 9th R. Innis. Fusrs. 2nd Lt. H.H. Lindsay & 9 O.Rs. proceeded to Divisional Signal School. Church Parades, and Inspections by Company Commandant. Reveille at Tarq in the afternoon.	
-do-	10/7/17		2nd Lt. J.G. Bailey & 2 O.Rs. proceeded to Army School at LE TOUQUET.	

WAR DIARY
of
10th R. Innis. Fus. INTELLIGENCE SUMMARY.

Army Form C. 2118.

(Erase heading not required.)

Place	Date	Hour	Summary of Events and Information	Remarks and references to Appendices
HAUT LOQUIN	10/7		Inspections at 9 a.m. Battalion Attack practice in the forenoon. Recreational Training in the afternoon.	
-do-	11/7		Maj. W. S. S. Reid proceeded to CALAIS as Draft Conducting Officer:- Aug. 109th Bgde. S.C. 1/2. Maj. Lieut. E.O. McCleatchie returned from Signalling School. Training as usual. A Reading & Writing Room has been opened in the Village School for the Battalion Use.	
-do-	12/7	20 R.'s.	Draft arrived from Base Depot. There was a Battalion parade at 10 a.m. under Major R.S. Knox D.S.O. Sports and prizes for the winners were observed. At 6 p.m. a Singing Competition was held and prizes were given. The judge was 2/Lieut. O.L.S. & C. Smith, who in civilian life was organist in Leeds Cathedral.	
-do-	13/7		Inspections Parades as usual in the forenoon. Recreational Training in the afternoon.	
-do-	14/7	12 Ot's.	Runners, Signallers & Linesmen have attended to Bgde. H.Q. for Special Instruction. The Battalion Football Team played the 109th F.A. team this evening. The Battn. team won by 4 Goals to 2.	

Army Form C. 2118.

WAR DIARY
of 10th R. Innis. Fus.

INTELLIGENCE SUMMARY.
(Erase heading not required.)

Instructions regarding War Diaries and Intelligence Summaries are contained in F. S. Regs., Part II. and the Staff Manual respectively. Title pages will be prepared in manuscript.

Place	Date	Hour	Summary of Events and Information	Remarks and references to Appendices
HAUT LOQUIN	15/7		Maj. H. A. Lulias returned from Supply Course. There was a Bugle Band Service in ALQUINES at 11.30 a.m. After which Military Medal ribbons were Presented to the men recently awarded by the Divisional Commander. Lt. Moore was given an extension of leave to the 5th inst. by a Medical Certificate. Parades etc. as usual.	
-do-	16/7		Inspection of Attack practice as usual. Rec. Training in the afternoon. The Field Marshall, Commander-in-Chief has been authorised by His Majesty the King to award Decorations to the following:– Military Cross to Maj. J. McMeekan, Maj. R. Patterson, and Capt. S.E. Picken (R.A.M.C. attached) D.C.M. to N°. 24768 Cpl. E. Beare (Batn. Scout N.C.O.)	
-do-	17/7		Maj. O.H. Picken is attached or Batn. Strength today. 13357 Pte. Capel H.P. r 27935 Pte. Reid N. are transferred to 233rd. Employment Company from this date. Training as usual.	

86

Army Form C. 2118.

WAR DIARY
of
10th R. Innis. Fus.
INTELLIGENCE SUMMARY.

(Erase heading not required.)

Instructions regarding War Diaries and Intelligence Summaries are contained in F. S. Regs., Part II and the Staff Manual respectively. Title pages will be prepared in manuscript.

Place	Date	Hour	Summary of Events and Information	Remarks and references to Appendices
HAUT LOQUIN	18/7	—	15 O.R.s Draft joined today. 2nd Lt. J.W. Drennan rejoined Battalion from England and posted to "C" Coy. A Brigade Scheme (Attack) was carried out today. See practice orders attached.	
— do —	19/7		D.S.O. Lt. Col. F.S.N. Macrory & Capt. A.F. Cook rejoined Battn. from Leave. No. 12 Platoon "C" Coy. gave a Demonstration of a Platoon Attack with Live Ammunition & Grenades at 6am. to the Battn. Lectures on Village Fighting were given by Coy. Commanders, and a practice was carried out afterward. Inspection of Rifles by Armr. Sgt. was carried out in the afternoon.	
— do —	20/7		1 O.R. transferred from 11th R. Innis. Fus. Capt. R.C. Hughes & 2nd Lieut. Knox proceeded with F.O.R.s to Divisional Depot Battn. & O.R.s proceeded to Army Rest Camp near BOULOGNE. Capt. E.A. Barton came to act as 2nd in Command and takes over Command of "D" Coy. 2nd Lt. Jamieson is reported to "D" Coy. Training as Usual.	

WAR DIARY
of 10th R. Innis. Fus.
INTELLIGENCE SUMMARY.

Army Form C. 2118.

(Erase heading not required.)

Place	Date	Hour	Summary of Events and Information	Remarks and references to Appendices
HAUT LOQUIN	21/7/17		2nd Lt. J. A. Crotley was granted leave to U.K. 14th inst. A Batt. Scheme was carried out on Batt. Training Ground.	
-do-	22/7/17		Church Service.	
-do-	23/7/17		1 O.R. to Army Cookery School. 2 O.Rs. to Brigade Intelligence. 2nd Lieut. A. Patterson proceeded on Intelligence Duties to the Line.	
-do-	24/7/17		5 O.Rs. Dept reported Batt. 1 O.R. taken gas with 9th Batt. 2nd Lt. P.H. Dickin returned from sick leave. Capt. Baird 7 O.Rs. proceeded to U.K. on leave. Attack practice as usual	
-do-	25/7/17		Training as usual. See Opsoions Orders of 24.7.17.	
-do-	26/7/17		2 O.Rs. Dept reported, 2 O.Rs. to Lewis Gun School at LE TOUQUET. The Batt. marched from HAUT LOQUIN at 11 a.m. today, marching 5 kilometres they entrained on Busses and arrived about	

WAR DIARY
of
10th R. Innis. Fus.rs
INTELLIGENCE SUMMARY.

Army Form C. 2118.

(Erase heading not required.)

Place	Date	Hour	Summary of Events and Information	Remarks and references to Appendices
WINNEZEELE AREA.	26/7/17		10.p.m. in WINNEZEELE, and marched to Camp at J. 11.	
	27/7/17		Maj. A. Patterson returned to-day. Battalion Kit Inspection by C.O.	
-do-	28/7/17		Attack Scheme. Lee attacked Advanced & offer. Divs. 2/Capt. Ritter & 6 O.R.s. proceeded on Leave.	
-do-	29/7/17		1 Offr. from 11th Battn. Inf. Lt. W.C. Griffiths proceeded to Bgde. on Staff Duty & 2 Lt. O.C. Snee took over duties of a/Asst. Gas School Instr & Inspector.	
-do-	30/7/17		Maj. L. McMeekan & 2 O.R.s. proceeded to U.K. on Leave. The Battalion travelled to HIPHOEK (near Poperinghe) today, arriving there at 2 a.m. 31/7/17.	
HIPHOEK -do-	31/7/17		Maj. L. Knox returned from 102 Divisional Reserve Battn. 8 O.R.s. to 109th M.G. Coy. for attachment.	

Army Form C. 2118.

WAR DIARY
of
INTELLIGENCE SUMMARY. 10th R. Innis. Fus. S.

(Erase heading not required.)

Instructions regarding War Diaries and Intelligence
Summaries are contained in F. S. Regs., Part II.
and the Staff Manual respectively. Title pages
will be prepared in manuscript.

Place	Date	Hour	Summary of Events and Information	Remarks and references to Appendices
	1st July. 1914.		Batn. Strength Comp and. O. O.R.'s O. O.R.'s With Battalion. 30 777 31 768 On Command. 4 62 3rd July. 1914. 3 75 On Leave. 3 20 3 24 In Hospital. 3 39 2 28 40 898 39 898 H.H.Mulcahy. Lieut. Colonel, Comm'd'g. 10th (S.) Battn. Royal Inniskilling Fusiliers.	

S E C R E T.   Copy No.
10th Battalion Royal Inniskilling Fusiliers

Map References
HAZEBROUCK 5 A (Edition 2). & CALAIS 1/100,000.   24th JULY, 1917.
----

1. The WHITE Force (enemy) had been driven into the B de CONDETTES, and is retiring westward on BOULOGNE.
   Our present Outpost line runs :- BONNINQUES Station E. Edge of B de CONDETTES - HERICAT - Second N in FORET NATIONALE.

2. The 10th Royal Innis. Fusiliers with the 9th Royal Innis. Fusiliers on right and 11th Royal Innis. Fusiliers on Left, will act as Advance Guard to the L.... Division, from 9.30 a.m. 25/7/17, and will advance from Outpost Line, with its left flank resting on road running through L of HERICAT and B of B de TERTRE on a frontage of 630 yards, to seize high ground running S.E. from second E of LE POIRIER to point where the above road crosses the ridge.

3. The Battalion will rendezvous at 9.20 a.m. 25/7/17, with head of column at the cross roads N. of the T of HERICAT, facing S.W.

4. The Battalion will parade ready to march off at 7 a.m., with head of column at H of Hte PLANQUE, in fighting Kit without haversacks or Steel Helmets. Each man to carry 10 rounds blank ammunition. Flares to be carried by Section Commanders. A certificate will be rendered to the Adjutant before the Battalion moves, by each Company and Specialist Detail, that no one is in possession of any Ball ammunition or bombs. Order of march :- "A", "B", "C", "D" Companies. Scouts and Signallers. Haversack Rations will be carried and full water bottles.

5. The ground between the road which passes through the L of HERICAT and first E of BOIS du TERTRE and the road from HERICAT Village through the second E of B du TERTRE is inundated and impassable.

6. A Contact Aeroplane will be in the air from 10 a.m. and flares will be lit by front line troops when called for by Aeroplane by Klaxon Horn or White Very Light.

7. The Battalion will advance with 2 Companies, "C" & "D" in advance, and 2 Companies "A" & "B" in Support. ("C" & "A" Companies on right). The left will direct.
   Each Company (less 1 Reserve Platoon of each Coy.) will advance on a 2 platoon front, with 1 platoon in support. Each Company will send strong Officers Patrols in advance of the leading line to reconnoitre and report enemy's positions.
   Time is a most important factor, and enemy Machine Guns etc., <u>must</u> be dealt with promptly, so as not to unduly delay the advance.
   Each Company is (as always) responsible for watching its own flanks, and must keep touch with Battalions on right and left.
   Artillery support (imaginary) may be called for if urgently necessary.
   The Reserve Platoons of Each Company will report to O.C. Battalion and will be detailed as Carriers and Battalion Reserve.

8. Transport Officer will detail 2 Double Limbers with S.A.A. and Bombs, tools and Signalling Stores to follow Battalion. These limbers on arrival at Rendezvous will be parted at the cross roads N of T in HERICAT, when troops move off and pack mules will be loaded from them. Battalion Transport Officer will report to Brigade Transport Officer for further instructions on arrival at rendezvous.

9. C.O. and Company Commanders will meet the Brigadier at head of column at 9.15 a.m., 25/7/17.

10. Reports to Battalion Headquarters which will move with Battalion Reserve in rear of the Support Platoons on the road forming left flank of Battalion. Its position will be indicated by the Battalion Battle Flag.

(Signed) F.S.N. MACRORY, Lieut-Colonel

NARRATIVE.

British Troops advancing East, have reached a line HOCQUINGHEM, SURQUES, ESCOUILLES, BRUMEMERT, QUESQUES, the position of the Germans is rather indefinite. The Outposts of the 109th. Brigade are on the spur ½ mile South East of ESCOEUILLES.

10th. (Service) Battn. Royal Inniskilling Fusiliers.

Map reference- CALAIS 13, 1/ 100,000   Order No.10.

INFORMATION. By aeroplane and Scouts it has been ascertained that the enemy about 2 Companies strong are dug in 50 yards East of track running South from F in Fm. to first T in Court HAUT, with a second line on the Western Edge of B FORTE TAILLE. The intervening ground being very rough and scrubby, almost impassable.

INTENTION. As a preliminary to a further advance the 10th Inniskillings will attack these two lines on a frontage of 200 yards, their right flank on the B COURTE HAUT and their left on B de LOQUIN.

INSTRUCTIONS. "C" & "D" Companies will attack the enemy front line, "C" Company on right, "D" Company on left, each on a one Platoon Frontage, each using three platoons and detailing there Reserve Platoon to Battalion Reserve. Line when taken to be consolidated. "A" & "B" Companies will pass through when "C" & "D" Companies have gained their objective and take the enemy second line, "A" Company on left, "B" Company on right, which they will consolidate. Battalion will be in position at 9.30 a.m. ready for the signal to attack.

DIRECTION. Magnetic Bearing 122°.

FLARES. Will be lit on gaining objective when called for by Contact Aeroplanes.

SIGNAL OFFICER. Will make usual arrangements for relay of runners and signalling to Contact Aeroplanes, Battalion Headquarters and Brigade Forward Station.

MACHINE GUN COMPANY. 1 Section to co-operate under special orders.

TRENCH MORTAR BATTERY.   -- do --

Battalion Headquarters at bend in track 200 yards West of B in B de LOQUIN.

ESCOEUILLES - 6 a.m. by Conference, & confirmed by Runner at 6.30 p.m.

(Signed) F.S.N. MACRORY, Lt-Colonel,
Commanding 10th (S) Bn. Royal Innis. Fusiliers.

W A R   D I A R Y

10th Royal Inniskilling Fusiliers.

For Month of AUGUST 1917.

CONFIDENTIAL.

Army Form C. 2118.

WAR DIARY
of
INTELLIGENCE SUMMARY. 10th. Royal Irish Fusiliers.
(Erase heading not required.)

Instructions regarding War Diaries and Intelligence Summaries are contained in F. S. Regs., Part II. and the Staff Manual respectively. Title pages will be prepared in manuscript.

Place	Date	Hour	Summary of Events and Information	Remarks and references to Appendices
H.I.P.HOEK	1/7		Heavy rain all day. Preparations for the coming advance were continued. Battalion remained in billets. Divisional cards were issued to 12 N.C.Os. and men of Battalion for gallantry on 1st. July, 1916 and 4th. June 1917. S.O.Rs Staffordshire Batts. from 2a. (48th) Div. Base Depot. 4 Lt. J.M. Bennett & 25 O. Rs. proceed to 150 th. Coy R.E. for duty during active operations. See order attached A-1/8/17.	
-do-	2/7		Heavy rain all day. Major Venn, D.S.O. Intelligence Officer, Signalling Officer, Transport Officer & Coy. Officers reconnoitred the ground to gain information re the coming offensive. 10. O. Rs. proceeded to U.K. on leave.	
-do-	3/7		Rain continued all day. Coy Officers & N.C.Os. attended a Picture given by the Intelligence Officer bearing on the coming advance.	
-do-	4/7		The Battn. moved to VLAMERTINGHE (H.9.c.8.7.) at 7.30 a.m. where they were accommodated in Bivouacs & Huts.	

WAR DIARY
or
INTELLIGENCE SUMMARY.

10th Regt. Irish Fusiliers.

Army Form C. 2118.

(Erase heading not required.)

Place	Date	Hour	Summary of Events and Information	Remarks and references to Appendices
VLAMERTINGHE	5/8/17		Bright sunshine all day. Enemy shelled the Dumps about 400 yds N.E. of Camp.	
			Capt. Cott proceeded the Plain pending his departure to the Indian Service and is relieved of Batta. Establishment accordingly. 2nd Lt. T.W. May left for Army Rest Camp BOULOGNE with party of 3 O.Rs.	
			Church Service at 11 a.m.	
-do-	6/8/17		A meeting of Battalion Commanders & 2nds-in-Command of the Brigade was held at Batt. H.Q. Mess. Brigadier-General A. Richards presiding.	
			10 O.Rs. proceeded to U.K. on Leave.	
-do-	7/8/17		During the forenoon two inspections were held by Bgy. Commander. All deficiencies were made up as far as was possible.	
			The Battn. marched out of Camp at 8 p.m. proceeding via YPRES, WIELTJE, they relieved the 15th Royal Irish Rifles in a Support line (see Map Orders attached) Relief was completed by 1 a.m. 8/8/17. During relief Enemy's Artillery was very active, one Company suffered with Rev. Shell (Minefield) 5 men were killed & about 20 O.Rs. were gassed & sent to Field Ambulance. Our Artillery, especially the Heavy Guns were extremely lively.	

Army Form C. 2118.

WAR DIARY
of
INTELLIGENCE SUMMARY. 10th Royal Innis: Fusiliers.

(Erase heading not required.)

Instructions regarding War Diaries and Intelligence Summaries are contained in F. S. Regs., Part II, and the Staff Manual respectively. Title pages will be prepared in manuscript.

Place	Date	Hour	Summary of Events and Information	Remarks and references to Appendices
YPRES.	8/7		The enemy all intervals Shelled the front line & supports, also Bass Reserve (Batt. Headquarters) The Shells are mostly H.E. of large calibre with a few for Shrapnel and armour piercing Shells. The total Casualties including last nights are :- 2 O.Rs. Killed, 24 O.Rs. gassed and 18 O.Rs. wounded. "B" Company suffered very heavily in casualties.	
YPRES.	9th		The Battn. relieved the 9th R. Innis. Fusilrs. in the front line about midnight. During the day enemy's artillery was still extremely busy. At regular intervals he Shelled Bass Reserve & put a barrage on the WIELTJE Road. Our Casualties were :- 2 Killed, 6 Gassed & 14 wounded.	
YPRES.	10th		Between 4 & 5 a.m. the enemy put a barrage on our Front line. Our Artillery retaliated effectively. All day enemy Aircraft were very busy, during the day 2 of our Aeroplanes were forced to land in far on the enemy's line and one in No Mans Land quite convenient to an O.P. & 2 of our O.P. then were driven down by the enemy. The Gassoms of each side were raised during the greater part of the day. Our Casualties to day were :- 2/Lt. A. Boyd, Regt. Sergt. Majort. Sgt. Sinclair. Killed. 2/Lt. C.A. McClatchie severely wounded (he died in Hospital 11/8/17) 2 O.Rs. gassed. 10 O.Rs. wounded. 10 Oth. RanRs. proceed to U.K. on leave.	

WAR DIARY
of
INTELLIGENCE SUMMARY

Army Form C. 2118.

10th. Royal Irish Rifles

Place	Date	Hour	Summary of Events and Information	Remarks and references to Appendices
YPRES	11th.		Major R.S. Knox D.S.O. who had been in Command of the Battn. during the time was relieved to-day by Lt.-Col. J.S.H. Macrory D.S.O. Shelling still goes on at irregular intervals. A Patrol of the Rumford Scout came into our lines to-day, he had been wounded & wandered through No Mans Land since the Push on the 2nd inst. living on rations taken from the Dead Huns. Our Casualties to-day were:- 4 O.R's. Killed (Rfn J.W. Denman was wounded & died shortly afterwards) Lt. E.N. Macrory D.S.O. wounded & 18 O.R's wounded. Major Knox D.S.O. again proceeded to the trenches & took over Command of the Battalion.	
YPRES	12th.		The Battalion was relieved by the 15th. R. Irish Rifles in the Front Line to-day, relief commencing at 11.45 p.m. Relief was completed at 2 a.m. 13/8/17. The Battalion retiring to VLAMERTINGHE camp through WIELTJE & YPRES. They were joined by the details left behind at B.H.Q. Line Transport, 6 Lewis guns, Artillery was quiet during relief and the Battn. proceeded without a Casualty.	
VLAMERTINGHE	13th.		The Battn. is recuperating to-day, after a hard time in the line.	
—do—	14th.		Kit Inspections were carried out during the forenoon by Platoon Commanders. Deficiencies were indented for. 10 O.R's proceed to U.K. on leave. 2 O.R's wounded on 11th & 12th insts. Died of Wounds in Hospital. New Operation Orders attached I.C.R.4. Army School & 4 O.R's to Divisional School.	

WAR DIARY
INTELLIGENCE SUMMARY

Army Form C. 2118.

of 11th. Royal Irish Rifles Festubert.

(Erase heading not required.)

Instructions regarding War Diaries and Intelligence Summaries are contained in F. S. Regs., Part II. and the Staff Manual respectively. Title pages will be prepared in manuscript.

Place	Date	Hour	Summary of Events and Information	Remarks and references to Appendices
VLAMERTINGHE	15th.		Fighting kit was overhauled. Tea, sugar and chocolate, lemons etc. were issued. Capt. J. Gaston. M.C. Chaplain held a Batt. Service at 11 a.m. At 8.30 p.m. the Batt. moved up to their assembly positions in our old Support Line (Pinigan Garden & Congrew Trench) 800 yds. west of WIELTJE. Movement by platoons via YPRES. Salvation Corner, Canal Bank, Track 6. A few shells were put clear of us but no Batt. casualties were suffered. Lieutho were taken over at 1 a.m. 16/8/17. Batt. H.Q. in WIELTJE dugout. Major R.S. Knox, D.S.O. in command. The 10th of Batt. in G. (reserve) of advance to Brigade Reserve. It was at Zus to Black Line.	
-do-	16th.		At Zero Time 4.45 a.m. all troops reported they were on the move. A, B, C & D Coys. to assault positions in the Black Line (old enemy 2nd System) & Coy. to our old front line to remain at Bat. Major advance for carrying. 30 minutes later all were reported passing over old front line. At 5.50 a.m. Brigadier ordered Batt. H.Q. to move forward to vicinity of Spree Farm which was reached at 6.55 a.m. On arrival there, from stalwarts of wounded it was found enemy had held up leading Battalion Veruna Pond farm & the Brigade on our right on our left were being driven off Hill 35. This was reported to Brigade by runner & orders received to organise Black line & hold it at all costs. This was carried out. Most of the men being pushed forward into old trenches in front of Black Line which was followed as the enemy put a continual barrage on dugouts in Black line during whole day. 2/Lt. R.O. McConnell went forward with two Lewis Guns to help 14th R. Irish Rifles retake Clean Point 66 east of Spree	

Army Form C. 2118.

WAR DIARY
of
INTELLIGENCE SUMMARY. 10th Bn. Royal Inniskilling Fusiliers

(Erase heading not required.)

Instructions regarding War Diaries and Intelligence Summaries are contained in F.S. Regs., Part II. and the Staff Manual respectively. Title pages will be prepared in manuscript.

Place	Date	Hour	Summary of Events and Information	Remarks and references to Appendices
VLAMERTINGHE	16th		Fairly cold & dull all day. The Battalion was relieved during the night by 8th R. Irish Rifles. Relief being completed at 5.30 a.m. 17/8/17. 2/Lieut Spain was killed & 4 O. Ranks & 59 Wounded & missing. All ranks behaved with the greatest coolness during a trying time & there were many acts of heroism in attending to wounded, carrying messages, etc. "E" Company joined the Battn. in Black Line during the fore-noon.	
—do—	17th		The Battn. moved to WINNEZEELE area at 4 p.m. by Buses. 2/Lieut A. Patterson was admitted to Hospital "Sick" 15/8/17. The Divisional Commander Approved of the following Officers wearing the Badge of Rank R Staves, pending the receipt of Official Confirmation:- Y. Captain F.H. Barton — Major Y. Lieut. A.M.H. MacR — Captain Y.Y.Lieut. F.W. Davidson — Lieutenant Y.Y.Lieut. A. Patterson — Lieutenant	
WINNEZEELE	18th		Kit Inspection was held to day. Enemy Aircraft was heard over head during the night. 10 O. R. Proceeded to U. K. on Leave.	

Army Form C. 2118.

WAR DIARY
of
INTELLIGENCE SUMMARY. 1o A. Royal Inniskilling Fusiliers.

(Erase heading not required.)

Instructions regarding War Diaries and Intelligence Summaries are contained in F. S. Regs., Part II. and the Staff Manual respectively. Title pages will be prepared in manuscript.

Place	Date	Hour	Summary of Events and Information	Remarks and references to Appendices
WINNEZEELE	19th		A Brigade Church Service was held at 11 a.m. The Brigadier General afterwards addressed the Brigade. The Divisional Band was in attendance. 3 O.Rs. wounded have since died of wounds in Hospital.	
-do-	20th		No Orders attached. Platoon Drill in the forenoon. Recreational Training in the afternoon. 45 O.Rs. Rank & File joined 15 day from 30th Div Reserve Battn.	
-do-	21st		Platoon Drills in the forenoon. Recreational Training in the afternoon. 2 Lieut. H.W. Jamieson & 8 N.C.O's proceeded to BAPAUME to take up Billets in HARINCOURT for the Battn.	
-do-	22nd		Battn. Parade at 11 a.m. under Major Lunn, D.S.O. 10 O.Rs. proceeded to U.K. on Leave also Capt. A.M.H. Marr. A cricket match was held with 14th R.I. Rifles (Y.C.V's). This Bn. won by 49 [runs] to nil.	
-do-	23rd		Parade & Training as usual. Camper Billets were cleaned. C.O.'s Inspection at 7 p.m. Kit was packed & loaded ready for early turn to move.	

Army Form C. 2118.

WAR DIARY
of
INTELLIGENCE SUMMARY. 10th Royal Innis-Killing Fusiliers.

(Erase heading not required.)

Instructions regarding War Diaries and Intelligence Summaries are contained in F.S. Regs., Part II. and the Staff Manual respectively. Title pages will be prepared in manuscript.

Place	Date	Hour	Summary of Events and Information	Remarks and references to Appendices
WINNEZEELE	24th		The Battalion moved out of camp at 1.30 a.m. marched to CAESTRE, where they had Breakfast at 4.30 a.m. Entraining began at 6 a.m. and all was ready to move off at 6.45 a.m. The regiment was entrained in twelve Wagons. Arriving at BAPAUME Station at 4 p.m. they marched about 5 Kilometres to HAPLINCOURT, led by Billeting Party, where a Camp comprising NISSEN huts & Tents awaited them, being vacated by S. STAFFORDS.	
HAPLINCOURT	25th		Platoon & Company Drill with Recreational Training intervening. Reconnoitring Parties went to view the Front line & Supports. The Bn. beat the 1st R. Ir. Rifles at Football by 3 goals to nil.	
-do-	26th		Church Service was held. 1 Officer & 4 O.Rs. proceeded to U.K. on leave. Bathing Parade was also held.	
-do-	27th		Coy. & Platoon Drill & Lewis Gun Instruction was carried out. 2/Lieut. J.A. Casey took over duties of Q/Mar. vice 2/Lt. Small. A draft of 116 O.Rs. proceeded from 36th Div. Base & joined the Batt. this evening	

Army Form C. 2118.

WAR DIARY
of
INTELLIGENCE SUMMARY. 10th Royal Inniskilling Fusrs.

(Erase heading not required.)

Instructions regarding War Diaries and Intelligence Summaries are contained in F. S. Regs., Part II. and the Staff Manual respectively. Title pages will be prepared in manuscript.

Place	Date	Hour	Summary of Events and Information	Remarks and references to Appendices
HAPLINCOURT.	28th.		Capt. C.U.R. Sturge was admitted to Rear Camp (tempy) to day. Battn. moved to YTRES Area to day at 2.30 p.m. Distance covered 5 kilometres.	
YTRES AREA	29th.		The Battalion moved to BERTINCOURT at 8.30 a.m. The village is almost level, the boys were billetted in huts mostly. Some in Dieuts.	
BERTINCOURT.	30th.		Battn. Inspection etc. Clean parades & Platoon Drill were carried out. Working parties were instructed to repair Dieuts etc. Two working parties were also sent up the line, everything all right & returning at 4 a.m. A Staff of 7 O.R's arrived to day. 7 R. Inniskns rejoined the Battn. to day.	
—do—	31st.		Working Parties continues. Parades etc. were also continued. A football match between 10 R. Inn. Fus. & 9 th. R. Innis. Fus. took place near the village. The result was a draw - 2 goals each.	

WAR DIARY
OR
INTELLIGENCE SUMMARY.
(Erase heading not required.)

Army Form C. 2118.

Instructions regarding War Diaries and Intelligence Summaries are contained in F. S. Regs., Part II. and the Staff Manual respectively. Title pages will be prepared in manuscript.

Place	Date	Hour	Summary of Events and Information	Remarks and references to Appendices
			Summary of Strength etc. during August 1917:-	
			O.s W.O.s O.R.s	
			With Battalion 30 4 739	
			On Command 4 - 119	
			On Leave 3 - 25	
			In Field (Ambulance) 2 - 19	
			Attached (for rations) A.S.C. - - 1	
			Total 39 4 903	
			O.s W.O. O.R.s	
	31st Aug '17		27 3 579	
			1 38	
			3 1 50	
			3 - 35	
			- - 8	
			34 4 710	

Willis. Lt. Colonel.
Commdg 10th (Service) Bn. R. Innis. Fus.

1:10 000 G.3.

Position of Coys & Bn. H.Q. on morning of 16th Aug. 1917

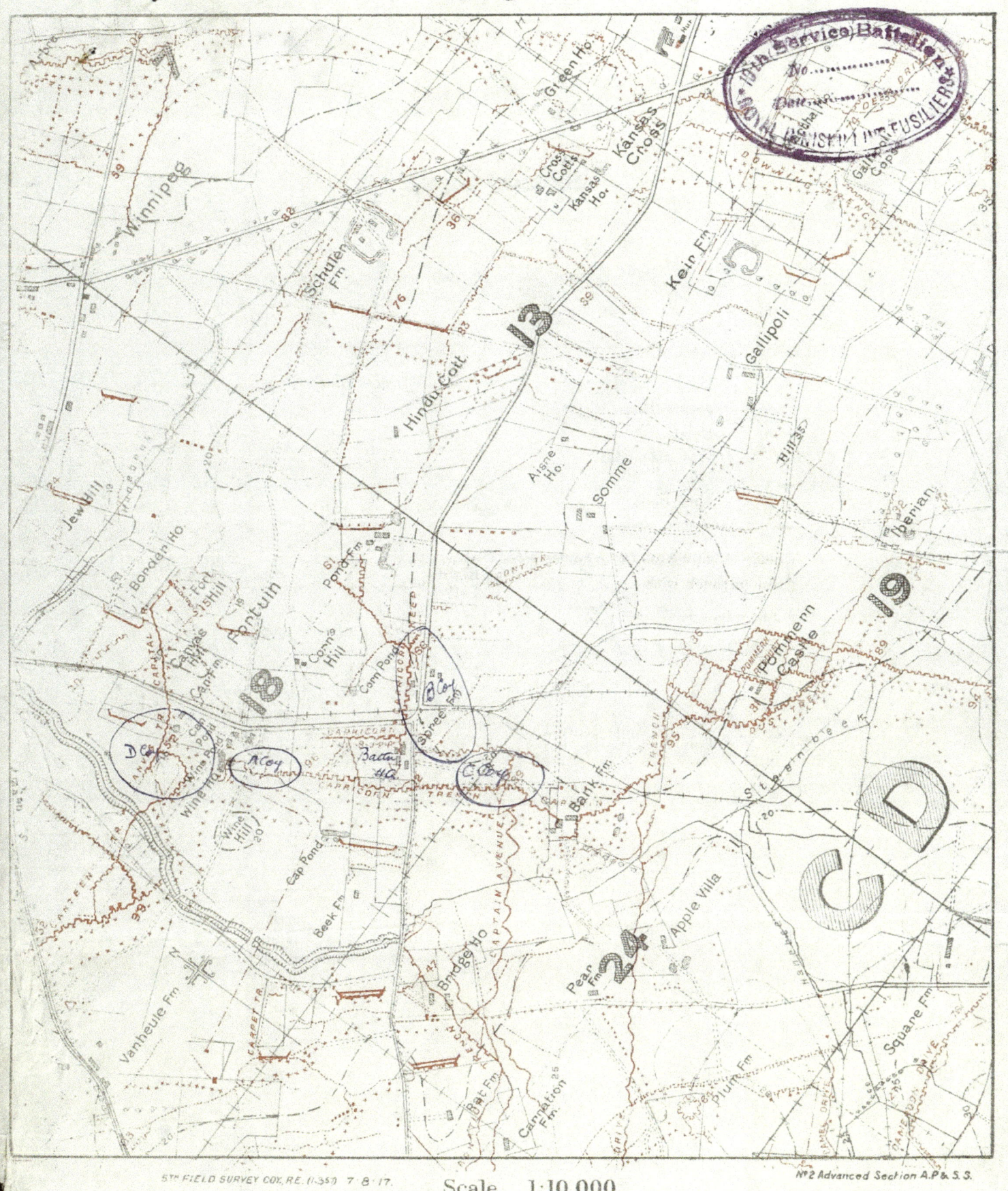

Scale. 1:10,000.

Message Form.

.............Division.

Map reference or mark own position on Map at back.

I am at................................

I am at................................and am consolidating.

I am at................................and have consolidated.

I need :—Ammunition.
- Bombs.
- Rifle Grenades.
- Water.
- Very lights.
- Stokes shells.

Enemy forming up for counter attack at...............................

I am in touch with....................on Right / Left at...............................

I am not in touch on Right. / Left.

Am being shelled from...............................

I estimate my present strength at.............rifles.

Hostile { Battery / Machine Gun / Trench Mortar } active at...............................

Time   a.m. (p.m.)   Name..............................

Date........................   Platoon........... Company...........

Place..............................   Battalion..............................

U.X.I. BRIGADE.

1. My position is marked ———
2. Position of other units is marked
3. Position of Enemy is marked **X X X X X X**
4. Position of Enemy M.G. holding me up **·/·**
5. Position of Enemy S.P. holding me up
6. My patrols have reached **P**
7. I have put out Outposts at ◇
8. I am pushing on to –/–/–/–/–/–
9. Counter attack is forming up at **C A.**

Numbers to refer to Platoons

S.P.

Time —————— Date —————— 19——

Signed ——————

—————— Commanding —————— Platoon.
—————— Company.
OVER.] —————— Battalion.

From, Signed _____

                 Comdg. _____ Platoon.

                              Company.

                              Battalion _____

Time _____ Date _____ 19 __

1. I have (*not*) gained my objective.
2. I do (*not*) want reinforcements.
3. My casualties are Light. / Heavy.
4. I am (*not*) in touch with my Right.
5. I am (*not*) in touch with my Left.
6. Our Barrage is { High. / Short. / Right.
7. Enemy Art. Barrage is Heavy. / Light.
    and is on
8. Enemy M.G. Barrage is Heavy. / Light.
9. I want following Stores :—

REPORT.

Seen and passed to _____ H.Q.

Time _____

       Signature.   [OVER.

CONFIDENTIAL.

W A R   D I A R Y

of

10th BATTALION ROYAL INNISKILLING FUSILIERS

Period 1st September 1917.
to
30th September 1917.

Army Form C. 2118.

WAR DIARY
of 10th Royal Inniskilling Fusiliers
INTELLIGENCE SUMMARY.
(Erase heading not required.)

Place	Date	Hour	Summary of Events and Information	Remarks and references to Appendices
BERTINCOURT P.D.6.	Sept. 10th		The strength of the Battalion to-day is :—	
			Off. N.C.Os. O.Rs.	
			With Battalion 27 3 567	
			Detached 1 – 50	
			Hospital 3 – 30	
			On Leave. 3 1 49	
			Total. 34 4 696.	

Army Form C. 2118.

WAR DIARY
of 10th R. Inniskilling Fusiliers
INTELLIGENCE SUMMARY.
(Erase heading not required.)

Instructions regarding War Diaries and Intelligence Summaries are contained in F. S. Regs., Part II. and the Staff Manual respectively. Title pages will be prepared in manuscript.

Place	Date	Hour	Summary of Events and Information	Remarks and references to Appendices
BERTINCOURT	September 1st		Clean parades at 9 a.m. Working parties proceeded to HERMIES, other parties worked at repairing trench, etc.	
P.D.C.			2.O.Rs. transferred from 9th Bn. R. Innis. Fus. in exchange. Extract Rise No 8 of Appointments, etc. Temp. Lieut. K.M. Qeem (att. to Q.S.L. Army) for duty as Town Major, HARPONVILLE, 19th March 1916. He to accordingly Knock off Establishment of Battalion.	
			2nd Lieut. J.T.M. Bennett took over duties as Brigade Bath Officer to day.	
			2nd Lieut. J. McCaw is appointed Transport Officer vice Lieut. T.W. Orr to Hdqrs. Regt. R.W. Glass (16th R.J.R.) is attached as Quartermaster on probation.	
			"J" Coy. played "B" a football match to day the result being 2 goals each.	
	2nd		Parades + Working Parties as usual.	
			2/Lieut. J. Mitchell + 3 O.Rs. proceeded to 4th Army Musketry School.	
			2/Lieut. R.J. Fanning + 40 O.Rs. proceeded to Army Rest Camp.	
			A Brigade Church Service was held at P.Y.C. 39 to day at 11 a.m. At the conclusion of the Service the Divisional Commander conferred Decorations to Officers of the Brigade.	
			A football match between "C" + "D" resulted in favour of "D" Coy. by 3 goals to 1.	

WAR DIARY
of 10th Royal Inniskilling Fusrs.
INTELLIGENCE SUMMARY.

Army Form C. 2118.

(Erase heading not required.)

Place	Date	Hour	Summary of Events and Information	Remarks and references to Appendices
BERTINCOURT	3rd.		Parades & Working Parties as usual.	
			B.O.Rs. paraded to M.O. as usual. Right Half Battn v Left Half played a match to-day. Result 3 goals each.	
			10.R. Transport was wounded to-day, while lifting a Team R an explosion occurred, blowing the ponies off 3 of his fingers, left hand, tearing him over face, chest & arms with small pieces of shrapnel.	
do	4th.		Parades & Working Parties as usual.	
			The Corps Commander inspected the Battalion at drill to-day.	
do	5th.		Authority is given for the following officers to wear the badge of higher rank :-	
			Major R.S. Knox, D.S.O. — Lieut-Colonel.	
			Captain G. H. Barton — Major.	
			Enemy Aircraft are very busy, twice machines passed over the village but were soon turned by our A.A. Guns.	
	6th.		See Relief order attached.	
HERMIES.	7th.		Battn. H.Q. are in the village. Enemy shells HERMIES during the afternoon with a few 5.9's &	

WAR DIARY
INTELLIGENCE SUMMARY

of 10th Royal Inniskilling Fusiliers.

Army Form C. 2118.

(Erase heading not required.)

Place	Date	Hour	Summary of Events and Information	Remarks and references to Appendices
HERMIES.	7th.		Whizzbangs. A Patrol of 1 Off & 5 O.Rs. went out for listening & observation. Nothing of interest to report. 2/Lieut. Davidson & 9 O.Rs. proceeded on leave to-day.	
do	8th.		Our Artillery fired 20 rounds into HAVRINCOURT to-day at 10 a.m. Jerrard "Stand To" 7 p.m. Short bursts of Machine Gun fire from the enemy were carried out on our front line. Enemy also bombed K.20.a.10.40. with Light Trench Mortar. 10 Rec Rec Bombs were fired but no damage & was an enemy aeroplane parade our HERMIES but was turned by our A.A. Guns Mr Pallew. 2/Lieut. J.T.M. Dunnett & 5 men proceeded to 109 A. L.T.M. Battery and an Officer of the Battn. Strength. The Corps & Divisional An visited the line to-day with Divisional & Brigade Comm and us.	
do	9th.		Our Artillery shelled road running through K.15.a. effectively also put 10 rounds into HAVRINCOURT. Enemy Artillery exploded 20. 4.2's in vicinity of support at K.15.a. & K.19.c. also shelled HERMIES. Our Machine Guns fired in short bursts on HAVRINCOURT – HERMIES road (K. 25 A.T.) at 8.30 p.m. One rifle Grenade & 6 R.T.M. exploded on K.20.c.20.60.	

Army Form C. 2118.

WAR DIARY
of 10th Royal Inniskilling Fusrs.
INTELLIGENCE SUMMARY.

(Erase heading not required.)

Instructions regarding War Diaries and Intelligence Summaries are contained in F. S. Regs., Part II. and the Staff Manual respectively. Title pages will be prepared in manuscript.

Place	Date	Hour	Summary of Events and Information	Remarks and references to Appendices
HERMIES.	9th.		2/Lieut. P.W.A.B. Amos relieved 2/Lieut. J.T.M. Bennett yesterday at Divisional Baths.	
			2/Lieut. W.B. Griffiths took over duties at Divisional Headquarters relinquishing his duty at Brigade H.Q.	
As	10th.		Our artillery fired on April Heap at K.20.a.5.0. + K.20.c.75.65. and on HAVRINCOURT.	
			The enemy fired 4.25 on our line at K.19.K. + K.20.a. at 5.15 p.m. No direct hits were obtained. At	
			11.45 p.m. 4 rounds H.25 were fired on HERMIES.	
			Our Machine Guns fired several bursts on K.21.a.v.c. and in direction of K.15.central. An	
			enemy Machine Gun fired at 4.25 a.m. in Ripple Dub Ducks from direction of April Heap (K.20) At	
			4.45 a.m. 6 Rock Dub Dents fired on Iuneh at K.20.c.10.60. The direct hit was obtained. we	
			retaliated with Rifle Grenades.	
As	11th.		Our Artillery Shelled the bridge at K.21.a.80.30. Heavily at 3.30 p.m. At 11.30 a.m. several shots were	
			fired on K.21.a.80.30. The enemy's Artillery was quiet. At 12.45 p.m. a few shells (4.2s) were fired	
			on HERMIES.	
			The Machine Guns fired in short bursts on K.15.a & c while the enemy fired from April Heap at	
			K.20.c.65.45 on K.20.c.10.35 from 3 a.m. to 4 a.m.	

Army Form C. 2118.

WAR DIARY
of 10th Royal Inniskilling Fusiliers.
INTELLIGENCE SUMMARY.
(Erase heading not required.)

Instructions regarding War Diaries and Intelligence Summaries are contained in F. S. Regs., Part II. and the Staff Manual respectively. Title pages will be prepared in manuscript.

Place	Date	Hour	Summary of Events and Information	Remarks and references to Appendices
HERMIES	11th		At 10.45 p.m. 5 Pineapples were fired at post in P.6. One direct hit on parados at K.9.4.90.75 was obtained. Sniping quiet. At 11 a.m. 2 enemy planes crossed our line + were engaged by our A.A. Guns + driven back. An enemy patrol was reported near our wire at K.20.a.20.30. at 9 p.m. and was fired on by the sentry + disappeared. 1 Off + 7 O.Rs. went on Patrol for the purpose of fighting + examination. They went round about + came into our wire at K.20.a.20.30. from NO MAN'S LAND. There were no signs of wire cutting + no signs of enemy patrol. Shell holes + small trench were occupied. 2/Lt. A. Parkinson has been invalided to England "sick." 1 Off + 7 # O.Rs. proceeded on leave to day.	
At	12th		Enemy shelled HERMIES frequently during the day. A few rocket bombs were also fired on Aceta. Nothing much to report to day. A concertina was heard being played at the April Heaps. The players seemed to be travelling down the crag from the line.	

Army Form C. 2118.

WAR DIARY
of 10th Royal Inniskilling Fus.
INTELLIGENCE SUMMARY.
(Erase heading not required.)

Instructions regarding War Diaries and Intelligence Summaries are contained in F. S. Regs., Part II. and the Staff Manual respectively. Title pages will be prepared in manuscript.

Place	Date	Hour	Summary of Events and Information	Remarks and references to Appendices
HERMIES	13th		Our Artillery was very active during the day, while about 11.30 a.m. the enemy shelled the village with 4.2's. Capt. J.M.C. Wilson leaving joined Battalion to day in La Rue en Wingles and proc'd to "B" Coy.	
	14th		See Reig Orders attached.	
BERTINCOURT	15th		Rev. 1 Officer & 8 O.Rs. proceeded on leave to day.	
do	16th		Clean parades in the morning at 9 a.m. Working Parties provided by train to HERMIES, work was also carried on in the village. Practice firing good levels for the winter, etc. "B" Coy beat "A" at football to day by 5 goals to one. 2 Off. + 140 O.Rs (Draft) joined Batn. to day.	
do	17th		Parades & Working Parties as usual	
do	18th		Parades & Working Parties as usual. No. 15897 Q/Sgt J. McNutt has been awarded the Military Medal by the Field Marshal Commanding.	

Army Form C. 2118.

WAR DIARY
of 10th R. Inniskilling Fus.
INTELLIGENCE SUMMARY.
(Erase heading not required.)

Place	Date	Hour	Summary of Events and Information	Remarks and references to Appendices
BERTINCOURT	18th		...in to-day under authority granted by His Majesty the King. "A" Coy beat "C" Coy at Football to-day by 3 goals to 1 in a Knock-out Competition.	
do	19th		Parades & Working Parties as usual. 1 Officer & 6 O.Rs. proceeded on leave to-day. The Corps Commander inspected the Batt. to-day & was pleased by the fine turn out. "B" Coy beat a Company of the 9 R. Innis. Fus. at Football by 5 goals to nil in the Competition.	
do	20th		Parades & Working Parties as usual.	
do	21st		Parades & Working Parties as usual.	
do	22nd		Major Rid Finlam having taken over command of the Battalion to-day is to-day on the Strength. Major (A/Lt/Col.) R.S. Hunt. D.S.O. relinquishes the acting rank of Lieut. Colonel on ceasing to command the Battalion & takes over duties of Second in Command.	

Army Form C. 2118.

WAR DIARY
of 16th Royal Inniskilling Fusrs.
INTELLIGENCE SUMMARY.

(Erase heading not required.)

Instructions regarding War Diaries and Intelligence Summaries are contained in F. S. Regs., Part II. and the Staff Manual respectively. Title pages will be prepared in manuscript.

Place	Date	Hour	Summary of Events and Information	Remarks and references to Appendices
	22nd		Major E. H. Davis relinquishes the Acting Comd. of 2nd in Command and takes over Command of "C" Coy.	
			Capt. J. K. Ritter takes over 2nd in Command of "C" Coy. on ceasing to command a Company.	
			Right Half Battalion played the left half a football match the result being 2 to 1 in favor of the Right Half.	
HERMIES.	23rd		Enemy threw a few shells into the village this evening.	
			The weather is good & aeroplanes are active on both sides.	
			1 Off. & 7 O. Rs. proceeded on leave to-day.	
A.	24th		Very good day for Aircraft. Enemy's aeroplanes exceptionally busy, our planes are also active. At 5 p.m. an enemy plane flew low over our village towards BERTINCOURT and fired one of our planes it assume it was then driven back by our A.A. guns.	
			At 6 p.m. 14 of our planes crossed over the enemy lines & remained there for some time although heavily shelled by Bosch A.A. guns.	
			An enemy plane was heard at 10 p.m. passing over village in a westerly direction.	

Army Form C. 2118.

WAR DIARY
of 10th Royal Inniskilling Fusiliers

INTELLIGENCE SUMMARY.

(Erase heading not required.)

Instructions regarding War Diaries and Intelligence Summaries are contained in F. S. Regs., Part II. and the Staff Manual respectively. Title pages will be prepared in manuscript.

Place	Date	Hour	Summary of Events and Information	Remarks and references to Appendices
HERMIES	24th		From 10 p.m. to 12 midnight our artillery were very busy the enemy fired a few shells in retaliation.	
do	25th		Again the weather was favourable for aircraft & both sides were very active. Artillery quiet during the day, towards night enemy fired some shells into HERMIES.	
do	26th		The day is dull & bad for observation therefore very little activity in the air. The enemy shelled various places in & around the village, towards midnight the shelling increased & after our artillery bombarded the enemy fr. to an hour the shelling ceased. 1 O.R. wounded to day by shrapnel from recon. bomb. (See Relief Orders attached.)	
do	27th		Again the weather is bad for observation but towards sunset it became clear when our planes showed some activity. 2/Lieut. R.J. Fanning & 2/Lieut. R.B. McConnell have been awarded the Military Cross by his Majesty the King. Marshall commanding in chief under authority granted by his Majesty the King. 6 O.Rs. proceeded on leave to day. 4 O.Rs. proceeded to Third Army Rear Camps to day.	

Army Form C. 2118.

WAR DIARY
of 10th Royal Inniskilling Fusiliers.
INTELLIGENCE SUMMARY.
(Erase heading not required.)

Instructions regarding War Diaries and Intelligence Summaries are contained in F.S. Regs., Part II. and the Staff Manual respectively. Title pages will be prepared in manuscript.

Place	Date	Hour	Summary of Events and Information	Remarks and references to Appendices
HERMIES.	28th.		Air Activity normal.	
			3 O.R.s joining Batt. to-day from Divisional Reinforcement Depot Batt.	
			There is little Artillery fire from the enemy, our Artillery are quieter than usual.	
			2 N.C.O.s proceeded to Corps Rifle & Bayonet Course at BOVES.	
"	29th.		Aircraft activity increased on both sides.	
			The enemy shelled a village at intervals during the day.	
			Nothing much to report to-day.	
			Lieut. T.W. Dwyer proceeded to AUXI-LE-CHATEAU to-day to attend a course at Third Army Infantry School.	
			No. 16812 A/Sgt. Sinclair proceeded to Musketry School, HYTHE to-day on a course.	
			2nd Lieut. R.C. Hughes & 1 N.C.O. proceeded to Divisional Reinforcement Camp as Instructors.	
"	30th.		Very good day for Aircraft. The enemy's planes were especially busy during the morning planes passed our village twice but were turned by our A.A. Guns. Our planes showed more activity in the evening and crossed over the enemy's line several times.	

Army Form C. 2118.

WAR DIARY
of 10th Royal Inniskilling Fusiliers.
INTELLIGENCE SUMMARY.
(Erase heading not required.)

Instructions regarding War Diaries and Intelligence Summaries are contained in F. S. Regs., Part II. and the Staff Manual respectively. Title pages will be prepared in manuscript.

Place	Date	Hour	Summary of Events and Information	Remarks and references to Appendices
HERMIES	30th		Artillery quiet throughout the day, but after 9 p.m. there was some activity on both sides.	
			2 Officers & 4 N.C.O.s proceeded to Corps School Boxes to attend a Lewis Instruction Course.	
			2/Lieut H.C. Peake proceeded to Base Depot to-day to act as instructor until 10th Dec. 1917.	
do.	30th.		The Strength of the Battalion to-day is:-	
				Off. W.O. O.Rs.
			With Battalion.	24 3 605
			Detached.	9 - 95
			Hospital.	1 - 21
			On Leave	3 1 24
			Total.	34 4 746

Farhan
Lieut. Colonel.
Comdg. 10th (S) Bn. R. Innis. Fus.

Army Form C. 2118.

WAR DIARY
of 10th. Royal Inniskilling Fusiliers.
INTELLIGENCE SUMMARY.
(Erase heading not required.)

Place	Date	Hour	Summary of Events and Information	Remarks and references to Appendices
BERTINCOURT.	Octr. 1st		The strength of the Battalion to day is :—	
			Off. W.Os. O.Rs.	
			With Battalion 24 3 602	
			Detached 9 — 97	
			Hospital 1 — 21	
			On Leave 3 1 25	
			TOTAL. 37 4 745	

Army Form C. 2118.

WAR DIARY
of 10th (S) Bn. Royal Innis. Fus.
INTELLIGENCE SUMMARY

(Erase heading not required.)

Instructions regarding War Diaries and Intelligence Summaries are contained in F. S. Regs., Part II. and the Staff Manual respectively. Title pages will be prepared in manuscript.

Place	Date	Hour	Summary of Events and Information	Remarks and references to Appendices
BERTINCOURT	October 1st.		Rest.	
			1 Officer & 5 O.Rs proceeded on leave to day.	
			No. 13666 Sergt. J. Kilgan proceeded to United Kingdom to train for a commission.	
			1 Officer & 5 O.Rs. joined Divisional Reinforcement Camp and are taken on strength of Batt.	
			4 N.C.O.'s proceeded to Brigade N.C.O.'s Course.	
do.	2nd.		1 N.C.O. & 50 O.Rs. to Corps School, Boves, 3 for a course of Bombing, 3 for a course in Lewis Gun.	
			5 Officers & 18 O.Rs. proceeded by train to AMIENS for a days holiday.	
			Work was carried on in the village making Telephone Dugouts & Billets for the winter.	
			No. 13499 Sergt. D. Shaw proceeded to United Kingdom to train for a Commission.	
do.	3rd.		Working Parties as usual.	
do.	4th.		Working Parties as usual.	
			6 O.Rs. proceeded to Corps School, Boves for a Signalling Course.	
			"B" & "D" Coys. played in the Football Competition to day, the result being 3 to nil in favour of "D".	

Army Form C. 2118.

WAR DIARY
of 10tt (s) Bn. Royal Innis. Fusrs.
INTELLIGENCE SUMMARY.
(Erase heading not required.)

Instructions regarding War Diaries and Intelligence Summaries are contained in F. S. Regs., Part II, and the Staff Manual respectively. Title pages will be prepared in manuscript.

Place	Date	Hour	Summary of Events and Information	Remarks and references to Appendices
BERTINCOURT	5th.		Working Parties as usual.	
			Major R. O. Kerr D.S.O. & 5 O.Rs. proceeded on leave 15 days.	
			2/Lieut. O.C. Richards having joined Battn. is taken on the Strength.	
do.	6th.		Working Parties as usual.	
			1 N.C.O. proceeded to G.H.Q. School, Pt. Pol. for a Course in Assault, Physical & Recreational Training.	
			"C" Coy. played "D" Battery, 173rd Bde. R.F.A. in Brigade Football Competition. Result - Scoreless Draw.	
			2 O.Rs. joined on transfer from 11th Royal Innis. Training & are taken on the Strength.	
do.	7th.		Church Services were held in Brigade Theatre for C. of E's. & Presbyterians to day.	
			"C" Coy. again played "D" Battery, 173rd Bde. R.F.A. Result. "C" Coy. 4 "D" Battery 1.	
do.	8th.		2 officers & 9 O.Rs. proceeded by train to AMIENS for a days holiday.	
			(See Policy Orders attached)	

Army Form C. 2118.

WAR DIARY
of 10th Royal Inniskilling Fusiliers.
INTELLIGENCE SUMMARY.

(Erase heading not required.)

Instructions regarding War Diaries and Intelligence Summaries are contained in F. S. Regs., Part II. and the Staff Manual respectively. Title pages will be prepared in manuscript.

Place	Date	Hour	Summary of Events and Information	Remarks and references to Appendices
HERMIES	9th		Weather showery & stormy. No flying during the morning. From 4 p.m. to 6 p.m. a few of our 'planes did patrol work. Enemy Artillery more active than usual. Our Artillery very active during the night. 7 other Ranks proceeded on leave to-day.	
do.	10th		Again the weather is stormy but not so rainy. Our aeroplanes came out during the evening and did patrol work. Nothing much to report to-day.	
do.	11th		The weather is better to-day and there is more activity in the air. 2/Lieut. L. Morrison & 2/Lieut. J. Brunt joined Battn. to-day and are taken on strength. 14 O. Rs. joined to-day and are taken on Battn. Strength. 2 O. Rs. wounded to-day.	
do.	12th		Aircraft very active during the afternoon. 2 of our 'planes were over the SLAGG HEAP at	

Army Form C. 2118.

WAR DIARY
of 10th Royal Inniskilling Fusiliers
INTELLIGENCE SUMMARY.
(Erase heading not required.)

Instructions regarding War Diaries and Intelligence Summaries are contained in F. S. Regs., Part II. and the Staff Manual respectively. Title pages will be prepared in manuscript.

Place	Date	Hour	Summary of Events and Information	Remarks and references to Appendices
HERMIES	12th.	6.35 p.m.	Raid 9 of our Planes passed over enemy's line & remained there for ½ an hour although heavily shelled by A.A. Guns.	
			Enemy fired some shells into HERMIES during the afternoon.	
			Our Artillery were active during the day. (Intn: for Relief - See Relief Orders attached.)	
Do.	13th.		Enemy planes were active during the morning.	
		About 4.30 p.m.	A Squadron of our Planes were seen close to a German Air Squadron but no fight took place.	
			Enemy shelled track between village & our front line. Some rocket bombs were fired at intervals during the evening into front line.	
			Our Artillery were active during the night.	
			C.O. proceeded on leave to-day.	
Do.	14th.		Artillery quiet on both sides.	
			1. O.R. transferred to 9th R. Innis. Fusrs. is struck off strength of Battalion.	
			2 N.C.Os proceeded to Div. Gas School for a course to-day.	

Army Form C. 2118.

WAR DIARY
of 10th Royal Inniskilling Fusiliers
~~INTELLIGENCE~~ SUMMARY.

(Erase heading not required.)

Instructions regarding War Diaries and Intelligence Summaries are contained in F. S. Regs., Part II. and the Staff Manual respectively. Title pages will be prepared in manuscript.

Place	Date	Hour	Summary of Events and Information	Remarks and references to Appendices
HERMIES	15th.		Aeroplanes very active on both sides.	
			The enemy shelled at intervals during the morning. From 4.30 p.m. to 5.30 p.m. about 25 shells (5.9's) were fired on HERMIES. Several fell close to the road at J.29. & 10.30. One direct hit on house at J.29. Central was obtained.	
			Our artillery were very active during the night.	
do.	16th.		Enemy aircraft very busy during the morning.	
			Artillery quiet on both sides.	
			7 O.Rs. proceeded on leave to-day.	
			(See Relief Orders attached)	
BERTINCOURT	17th.		Rest.	
			4 N.C.Os. proceeded to Brigade N.C.Os. Class. 1 O.R. proceeded to PERONNE for a Course of Sanitation.	
			8 O.Rs. having joined Reinforcement Camp are taken on strength of Battalion	
			7 O.Rs. proceeded on leave to-day.	

Army Form C. 2118.

WAR DIARY
of 10th R. Inniskilling Fusiliers
INTELLIGENCE SUMMARY.
(Erase heading not required.)

Instructions regarding War Diaries and Intelligence Summaries are contained in F. S. Regs., Part II. and the Staff Manual respectively. Title pages will be prepared in manuscript.

Place	Date	Hour	Summary of Events and Information	Remarks and references to Appendices
BERTINCOURT	18th		W.R. was again carried out in village improving billets & making new ones.	
			5 O.Rs. joined Batt. from Reinforcement Camp to-day.	
			7 O.Rs. proceeded on leave to-day.	
			"D" Coy. played "D" Coy. 14th R. Irish Rifles in Brigade Competition, the result being	
			"D" Coy. 10th R. Innis Fus. 1. "D" Coy. 14th R. Irish Rifles nil.	
do.	19th.		Working parties as usual.	
			5 Officers & 18 O.Rs. proceeded to AMIENS for a days holiday.	
			3 O.Rs. having joined Reinforcement Camp are taken on strength of Battalion.	
			7 O.Rs. proceeded on leave to-day.	
			In the football Competition Brigade Headquarters beat to-day by 3 goals to 1.	
do.	20th.		Working parties as usual.	
			1 Officer & 60 O.Rs. proceeded to IV Corps School for Lewis Gun & Stokes Mortar Course.	
			Capt. J.T.C. Miller having joined Batt. to-day, is taken on the strength.	

Army Form C. 2118.

WAR DIARY
of 10th Royal Inniskilling Fusiliers.
INTELLIGENCE SUMMARY.
(Erase heading not required.)

Instructions regarding War Diaries and Intelligence Summaries are contained in F.S. Regs., Part II, and the Staff Manual respectively. Title pages will be prepared in manuscript.

Place	Date	Hour	Summary of Events and Information	Remarks and references to Appendices
BERTINCOURT.	20th.		Coys. Mr. Meechan, M.O. & Batman proceeded to 3rd. Army Rest Camp to-day.	
			Major R. A. Knox, D.S.O. & 8 O.Rs. proceeded by Bus to LOCRE, BELGIUM to attend Memorial Service of the Late Major W. Redmond, who died of wounds in an Wolie Motor Ambulance, received at MESSINES RIDGE Battle on 7th. June, 1917.	
do.	21st.		Working Parties as usual.	
			1 N.C.O. proceeded to Third Army School for a Musketry Course.	
			1 Other Ran R proceeded to a Cookery Course at IV Corps School.	
			After Church Service to-day the Divisional Commander presented ribbons to all soldiers in the Brigade who have won distinctions up to the present.	
do.	22nd.		Working Parties as usual.	
			2 N.C.O.'s proceeded to Divisional Gas School for a Course to-day.	
			1 Officer & 9 O.Rs. proceeded to AMIENS for a days holiday.	
			2 O.Rs. having joined Reinforcement Camp are taken on Strength of Battalion.	

Army Form C. 2118.

WAR DIARY
of 10th Royal Inniskilling Fusiliers
INTELLIGENCE SUMMARY.
(Erase heading not required.)

Instructions regarding War Diaries and Intelligence Summaries are contained in F. S. Regs., Part II. and the Staff Manual respectively. Title pages will be prepared in manuscript.

Place	Date	Hour	Summary of Events and Information	Remarks and references to Appendices
BERTINCOURT.	23rd.		Working Parties as usual.	
do.	24th.		1st O.Rs. joined Battn. to day from Reinforcement Camp.	
			2 O.Rs. proceeded to 3rd Army Musketry School, WARLOY, to day for a Course.	
			(See Relief Orders attached)	
HERMIES	25th.		Weather rainy + stormy. - No flying.	
			Artillery quiet on both sides.	
do.	26th.		Weather still unfavourable for aircraft.	
			Enemy artillery quiet.	
			Our Artillery showed much activity during the night.	
			2/Lt. T. Hamilton + 2/Lt. H. Wherry having joined to day are taken on Bn. Strength.	
do.	27th.		Weather better + Aeroplanes are very active on both sides.	
			Enemy's artillery was very active during the whole day, and our Artillery retaliated during the	

Army Form C. 2118.

WAR DIARY
of 10th Royal Inniskilling Fusiliers.
INTELLIGENCE SUMMARY
(Erase heading not required.)

Instructions regarding War Diaries and Intelligence Summaries are contained in F. S. Regs., Part II. and the Staff Manual respectively. Title pages will be prepared in manuscript.

Place	Date	Hour	Summary of Events and Information	Remarks and references to Appendices
HERMIES	27th.		night.	
			8 Other Ranks proceeded on leave to-day.	
do.	28th.		Several times during the morning our planes crossed over enemy's line & did patrol work.	
			No enemy planes observed. Nothing much to report to-day.	
			1 N.C.O. proceeded to Divisional Gas School to attend a Gas Course.	
			16 Other Ranks having joined Reinforcement Camp are taken on Strength of Battn.	
			8 Other Ranks proceeded on leave to-day.	
			Lt. ~~Thorpe~~ and four O.R. proceeded on leave today to Thiepval. Chillingworth	
do.	29th.		Our planes were again active during the morning.	
			The enemy shelled HERMIES at intervals during the day.	
			Our Artillery activity normal.	
			4 Other Ranks proceeded on leave to-day.	
do.	30th.		The enemy again shelled HERMIES with (5.9's)	
			Our Artillery were busy during the night.	

Army Form C. 2118.

WAR DIARY
of 10th Royal Innis-killing Fusiliers
INTELLIGENCE SUMMARY.
(Erase heading not required.)

Place	Date	Hour	Summary of Events and Information	Remarks and references to Appendices
HERMIES.	30.9.		Extract from List of Appointments No. 156:—	
			"The undermentioned to be Acting Captains (Additional) dated 20.9.17.	
			"Temp. Lieut. L.W. Boyce.	
			"Temp. 2/Lieut. L.W. Davidson."	
			5 Other Ranks joined Battalion to day from Reinforcement Camp.	
			8 Other Ranks proceeded on leave to day.	
do.	31.9.		Enemy aircraft exceptionally busy all day. Several times passing over our lines.	
			Our planes did Patrol Work throughout the day.	
			Enemy shelled listening Post at R.4. with 4.25 Howitzers, also shelled HERMIES.	
			Our artillery activity was normal.	
			No. 19055 L/Cpl. Grundle R. proceeded on a Course to IV Corps School, BOVES.	
			3 Off. & 9 O.Rs. proceeded for 2 days holiday to AMIENS.	
			8 Other Ranks proceeded on leave to day.	
			Hon. Lieut. & Q.M. R.W. Ross granted leave from 1st day to 21st. inst. p.v.r. under auy of IV Corps.	
			No. Q/248 d/- 22.10.17.	

Army Form C. 2118.

WAR DIARY
of 10th Royal Inniskilling Fusiliers
INTELLIGENCE SUMMARY.
(Erase heading not required.)

Place	Date	Hour	Summary of Events and Information	Remarks and references to Appendices
HERMIES	Oct/ur 31/17		The strength of the Battalion to-day is :-	
			Off. W.Os. O.Rs.	
			With Battalion. 32 4 600	
			Detached 8 - 83	
			Hospital 2 - 24	
			On Leave - - 68	
			TOTAL 42 4 775	

Fairburn Lieut-Colonel,
Commanding 10th R. Innis. Fus.

Army Form C. 2118.

WAR DIARY
of
INTELLIGENCE SUMMARY.
(Erase heading not required.)

Instructions regarding War Diaries and Intelligence Summaries are contained in F. S. Regs., Part II. and the Staff Manual respectively. Title pages will be prepared in manuscript.

Place	Date	Hour	Summary of Events and Information	Remarks and references to Appendices
ACHIET-LE-PETIT	1.12.17		The strength of the Battalion today is as follows:—	
			Off. W.O. O.R.	
			With Battalion 41 4 614	
			Hospital 3 — 23	
			On Leave 1 — 38	
			On Command 5 1 81	
			50 5 756.	

Army Form C. 2118.

WAR DIARY
of
INTELLIGENCE SUMMARY.
(Erase heading not required.)

Instructions regarding War Diaries and Intelligence Summaries are contained in F.S. Regs., Part II. and the Staff Manual respectively. Title pages will be prepared in manuscript.

Place	Date	Hour	Summary of Events and Information	Remarks and references to Appendices
ACHIET.le.PETITE.	1/12/17		In the morning companies reorganised and about 3.30 p.m. Battalion routed camp near Achiet le petite and marched to a field near BAPAUME. Where the night 1st/2nd was spent in tents which had been erected by the Advance party which had proceeded the Battalion. 2 Lt. J. Mitchell and 9 other ranks proceeded to United Kingdom on leave.	JMc
BERTINCOURT	2/12/17	9 a.m.	Orders to move were received. Battalion left camp in Achiet le petit and marched to BERTINCOURT which was reached about 2 p.m. Head Quarters moved into the billets previously occupied by them and remainder of Battalion was billeted in that portion of the village previously occupied by our C and D Companies.	JMc
		11 a.m.		
do.	3/12/17		Battalion reorganised once again and prepared for taking over in the line. Major Jones proceeded to front line to reconnoitre the area prepared to be taken over.	JMc
do.	4.12.17	9.30 a.m.	Battalion marched out of BERTINCOURT to HAVRINCOURT WOOD (Q15) proceeding via RUYAULCOURT and METZ. Arrived at Q.15. Piled arms and men had their dinners.	REF MAP GOUZEAUCOURT 1/20,000
		12.15 p.m. 1.15" 3"	Bomb, rifle grenades and extra S.A.A. notes were issued to men. Battn. moved off by platoons at 200 yards interval and proceeded via TRESCAULT, relieving a unit of 29th Division in R.1.b and R.2.a. Two field cookers were taken up to cook thus all Battn. was in at 7.30 p.m.	JMc
		7.30"	For Battn. and left on head at L 31 c 90.30. The Battn. was accommodated in 10 deep mined dug outs that room was very limited. The night 4/5" was quiet. When Battalion moved into line Quarter Master stores and transport were moved to camp at W13 a 90.90. (near FINS) Transport Officer remained at Q 15 with 27 pack animals and a dump of S.A.A. Bombs and Tools.	

WAR DIARY
INTELLIGENCE SUMMARY
(Erase heading not required.)

Army Form C. 2118.

Place	Date	Hour	Summary of Events and Information	Remarks and references to Appendices
4/4/17	4/4/17		Details left out of line consisting of 10 officers and 65 O.R. went to ETRICOURT.	
	5/4/17	9 am	Major R. I. Knox D.S.O. being in Command of Batt. (Commanding officer having had to remain at transport lines) proceeded to Brigade H.Q. in 32a and was there informed that Battn. had to take over the line in R4 and R5 that night. He then proceeded up to reconnoitre the line.	
		2.30 pm	At about this time the enemy began a heavy bombardment on our line in R4 5.10 and 33	
		2.45 "	Battn. "Stood to"	
		3 "	Major Knox on his way back from the line sent D Company to man trench in R3a and R3c as it looked very much as if the enemy was going to make a big attack. Bombardment began to die down.	
		3.20 "		
		4 "	Battn. "Stood Down" and had tea.	
		4.20 "	Returns for 6th wit. used.	
		5.20 "	Advance Party from 6th Division took over trenches.	
		6 pm	Battn. moved off by platoons to proceed to line to take over from 2/8 "Warwicks" 61 Division.	
		9 "	Bn arrived at new Bn. H.Q. (R3 & 90.20) after wandering about a good	

WAR DIARY
or
INTELLIGENCE SUMMARY

Army Form C. 2118.

Place	Date	Hour	Summary of Events and Information	Remarks and references to Appendices
			deal with a guide who was very uncertain of the way, luckily the night was clear & frosty. Lt T.W. May and 8 O.R. proceeded on leave	
	6.12.17	1.30 a.m.	Relief complete. 3 companies in front line & one in support. Things a bit uncertain as div.l. affair of 5th. the BOSCHE attacked 61st Div. and position has not been properly cleared up. Dispositions D.coy. on left of line. C coy. in centre. B coy. on Right. A coy. in support.	
			night fairly Quiet. Enemy patrol dispersed at 12.30 a.m. at L.35.c.8.2 by L.G.ammo.	
		8.0 a.m.	message from Bayads LS say that BOSCHE prisoner stated that an attack was to take place between 8 a.m. and 8.30 a.m.	
		8.20 a.m.	A Bombardment began on our right - being mostly on 9th R.IN.FUS sector.	
		8.40	B= "STOOD TO"	
		8.44	messages came in that BOSCHE were working up HINDENBURG SUPPORT line in R.9.b. and that the 9th IN.FUS. were getting short of bombs. A company of 14th R. IRISH. RIFLES was then sent up to support 9th IN.F. and a block formed at R.9.b. 60.80.	

WAR DIARY of 10th R. INNIS. FUS.

INTELLIGENCE SUMMARY

Army Form C. 2118.

Place	Date	Hour	Summary of Events and Information	Remarks and references to Appendices
	6.12.17		A lot of bombing went on all morning and all available men were occupied carrying up bombs from Brigade dump at R.3.d.10.70.	
		2.p.m.	At about this time No. 2 platoon A Coy. was ordered to cross the open and attack the enemy in trench at R.9.c.90.50. They left our trenches at about R.3.d.50.30 under 2/Lieut. NELSON and making a detour to the left, got into the Bosche trench alright. They found it strongly held. After driving the Bosche a good way back, they had to return to our lines having exhausted their bombs & being heavily bombed by the Bosche. They had done excellent work, having killed a large number of Bosche and brought back 2 prisoners. Their casualties were 4 wounded.	
			At about this time 2/Lt. SHEARMAN (A Coy) was shot through the shoulder by Bosche Treachery. 6 Bosche with a M. Gun stood up on their fire step, and held up their hands and gun. 2/Lt. SHEARMAN went out to accept their surrender but they at once fired on him. No. 24768 Cpl. E. BLAKE. D.S.M. who was with him, charged to shoot 2 of the team, they at once "cleared" & Cpl. BLAKE carried 2/Lt. SHEARMAN back to our trenches under heavy fire.	

Ref: Map
GOUZEAUCOURT
1/20,000

WAR DIARY of 10th R. INNIS. FUS.

INTELLIGENCE SUMMARY

(Erase heading not required.)

Army Form C. 2118.

Place	Date	Hour	Summary of Events and Information	Remarks and references to Appendices
	6.12.17	11 a.m.	BOSCHE appeared to have given up his attempt to bomb any further along HINDENBURG SUPPORT.	
		11:15 a.m.	B² "STOOD DOWN" & block having been established by 14th R. IRISH RIFLES at R.9.c.70.70 and one by 2Lt. WILLIAMS (A coy) at R.4.c.50.55.	
		12 Noon	B² "STOOD TO" as it was reported BOSCHE were preparing for counter attack. nothing came of this.	
			Intermittent shelling for rest of the day.	
			The Battalion was now holding a line running from R.4.c.50.53 to L.35.a.00.35. with 2 platoons of A coy. in BOSCHE gun emplacement at L.35.a.00.35 with 2 platoons of A coy. in trench in R.3.d.50.60. hedges about R.4.c central. remainder of A coy. in trench in R.3.d.50.60.	
		7 p.m.	A message from Brigade that left coy. area was to be handed over to 108th Brigade (2nd R. IRISH R.). Relief was arranged to take place at midnight but did not take place till 6 a.m. when D coy. were withdrawn to trench in R.3.d central 50.60 and the post of A coy. that had been in that trench was sent up to trenches in R.4.c central. 3 men of D coy. killed by a rocket bomb just before relief.	

Army Form C. 2118.

WAR DIARY of 10th (S) Bn R. INNIS. FUS:

(Erase heading not required.)

Place	Date	Hour	Summary of Events and Information	Remarks and references to Appendices
	7.12.17.		Night quiet, Bosche shelled back areas fairly heavily.	
		6 a.m.	11th R. INNIS. FUS: who had taken over from 9th R. INNIS. FUS. during the night began a bombing attack to drive the Bosche back from the trenches they had taken from 9th R.IN.F. on previous day, 2 stokes mortars co-operated with them.	
		9 a.m.	A. Coy: established communication with 11th R.IN.F. at R.J.d.85:00	
		10:30 a.m.	The Bosche did not put up much of a fight and at about 10:20 a.m. the 11th R.IN.F had established posts at R.10.a.50.70. R.10.c.30.50.9 R.10.c.25.20. & were in touch with the WARWICKS (61 Div.) on their right.	
		3 p.m.	Bosche reported to be massing in R.10.central. Our artillery put a very fine barrage down, & the Bosche did nothing!!! Night fairly quiet, Bosche shelled back areas heavily.	
	8.12.17.	a.m. 11:30	A quiet morning. Message arrived that Bosche was massing in R.10.d. artillery stopped any attempt at attack.	

M.F. Ref:
BOUZEAUCOURT.
1/20,000.

WAR DIARY of 10th R. WARS. F.O.S.

Army Form C. 2118.

INTELLIGENCE SUMMARY
(Erase heading not required.)

Place	Date	Hour	Summary of Events and Information	Remarks and references to Appendices
	8.12.17	Noon	Orders received that we had to hand over to 2nd Rifles the left of our line up to R.5.a.05.40. Relief to be complete by 3.p.m. This meant that we should hand the line over (s-right to 8/9 R.IR.R. with 2 companies in front line and 2 in support. An area was now chosen for left support coy. in R.4.s.30.20. and that part of the coy. that was relieved by 2nd R.I.R.R. was brought back there while back also coy. H.Q. the remainder of the coy. still in the line being under B. coy. for purposes of relief. OR A. coy. also extended his line to the left taking over some posts from B. coy. The line was held as follows when handed over. Right Front coy: from, R.3.d.90.00. to R.4.c.90.60. coy. HQ at R.4.c.65.60. Left Front coy: from, R.4.c.90.60. to R.5.a.05.40. coy. HQ at R.4.d.35.75. Left Right Support coy, in dyals R.4.a.30.20. coy. HQ. is a set of dugouts. Right Support coy. " " R.3.d.50.70. coy. H.Q. at R.3.8.50.50. Bn.H.Q. at R.3.6.90.10. R. Aid Post at R.4.a.30.20.	

WAR DIARY of 11th R. WNIS: Regt:

Army Form C. 2118.

(Erase heading not required.)

Place	Date	Hour	Summary of Events and Information	Remarks and references to Appendices
	9.12.17	a.m. 1.40	Relief Complete. Bn is now [s] an old trenches in Q.5.C.c.d. near TRESCAULT. Trenches were now in a very bad state - trenches having been a good deal of rain, mud knee deep in some places. On the way out 2Lt. J. HAMILTON B Coy: was killed by a shell and 3 other men wounded at the same time. Bn did not arrive in west area until 6.30 a.m. one of the most tedious journeys ever experienced by this Bn. accomodation very cramped a large number of the men sleeping in small rest shelters, and so if had been a wet night things were worse pleasant. During this tour in the line the casualties were, 1. Officer & 5. O.R. Killed 1. " " 22. O.R. wounded. During this tour in the line rations & water were brought up a pack animals to dump at R.3.C.10.70. & carried up from there by carry. The front line was only waist deep except where posts were, & then the	

Army Form C. 2118.

WAR DIARY of 10th R. INNIS. FUS.
INTELLIGENCE SUMMARY
(Erase heading not required.)

Place	Date	Hour	Summary of Events and Information	Remarks and references to Appendices
			Were digging it down to give head cover. Coy. H.Qrs had deep dugouts, but there were no dugouts or shelter along the line.	
			The following officers accompanied the B². into the line.	
			B². H.Q.	
			Major . R.S. KNOX. D.S.O. i/c and S.	
			Capt. C.N.L. STRONGE adjutant.	
			2Lt. R.B.M. IRWIN. Intge. Off²	
			" N. LINDSAY. sigº off²	
			CAPT. S.E. PICKEN.M.C. M.O.	
			" J.G. PATON.M.C. Chaplin.	
			A Company. B Company.	
			Capt: J. McMECHAN.M.C. Capt: S.M.H.MARK.	
			2Lt. W. NELSON. 2Lt. V. HAMILTON	
			2Lt. F.C. WILLIAMS. Lt. S.F. RICHARDS	
			2Lt. J. SHEARMAN. 2Lt G.I. PARKER	
			E Company. D Company	
			Major E.H. BARTON. a/Capt. F.W. DAVIDSON	
			2Lt. T. BROWN. 2Lt. F. CINNAMOND	
			" F.W. SENNINTON. " W. PRICE.	
			" E. SHARPLEY.	
			Commanding Officer and 2Lt. CASKEY w/dr. remained at Q.L. Store: CaplG: Miller, Boyd, Hope Baker	
			2/Lts Pickens, Lt: Col: Capt: Wilton, Lt. Boyle w/Capt Ritter were left at E.T.R. COURT with details.	

Army Form C. 2118.

WAR DIARY of 10th R. Innis. Fus.
INTELLIGENCE SUMMARY.
(Erase heading not required.)

Instructions regarding War Diaries and Intelligence Summaries are contained in F.S. Regs., Part II. and the Staff Manual respectively. Title pages will be prepared in manuscript.

Place	Date	Hour	Summary of Events and Information	Remarks and references to Appendices
	9/12/17		During the period 4th to 9th the Battn. Transport did most excellent work getting rations etc up to Battn. along roads and tracks continually shelled by the enemy. Their casualties were 4 men wounded, 2 horses wounded, 1 mule killed and 4 mules wounded. Their lines in HAVRINCOURT WOOD were continually under shell fire and on the 9th inst. the pack train was taken back to Transport lines near SOREL. On the evening of the 8th a shell burst on the Battn. ammunition dump at HAVRINCOURT WOOD and set a lot of S.A.A. on fire. A large number of men and mules were standing by at the time No. 15476 Cpl. J. Donald at once ran in. Formed up the burning box and carried it some distance throwing it down well clear of all ammunition etc. By his plucky act he undoubtedly averted several casualties as there were several thousand rounds of S.A.A. and about 1000 bombs in the dump. Lt: Col. Lord A.K. Farnham relieved Major R.S. Knox D.S.O. 2.O.C's proceeded on leave today. Company Commanders were relieved from the details in command today and the Capt. J.T.E. Miller taking over H. Coy. A/Capt T.W. Boyce M.C. taking over B Coy, Capt F.D. Boyd C.Coy and Capt J.M.S. Walker A.Coy.	y/b y/c y/d
	10.12.17		About Midnight on the 9th Brigade sent orders for working parties on the 10th. 100 men under Capt. Boyd proceeded to repair trench on Highland Ridge in the morning & a party proceeded in the enemy to the same work. The enemy shelled the trenches several times during the day but did not inflict any casualties.	
	11.12.17		Working Parties proceeded to the same place as on the 10th. Orders were received to vacate the trenches occupied by the Battn & to move to Metz.	

A5834 Wt. W4973 M687. 750,000 8/16 D.D.& L. Ltd. Forms/C.2118/13.

Army Form C. 2118.

WAR DIARY of 10th R. Innis. Fus ~~Intelligence~~
~~INTELLIGENCE SUMMARY.~~
(Erase heading not required.)

Instructions regarding War Diaries and Intelligence Summaries are contained in F.S. Regs., Part II. and the Staff Manual respectively. Title pages will be prepared in manuscript.

Place	Date	Hour	Summary of Events and Information	Remarks and references to Appendices
	11.12.17		The Battn. moved off by sections shortly after 3p.m. The working parties proceeded straight to METZ, from Highland Ridge, their packs having been taken down by the Transport. Dinners for the day working party were prepared at METZ received on arrival of the party.	
METZ	12.11.17		The day was spent in getting the men bathed & in bringing our Mobile reserve up to establishment. An observation balloon near METZ was attacked by an enemy aeroplane & an interesting fight ensued. The observers were forced to descend in parachutes but the balloon was not damaged. The enemy 'plane escaped untouched.	
"	13.11.17		About 1a.m. a wire was received from Brigade warning us that a prisoner taken from the enemy the previous evening had stated that the enemy were going to counter-attack in strength at 6:30am today & that the Battn. must be ready to move at short notice. Our guns put down a splendid barrage. Breakfasts were prepared early so as to be ready in the event of orders to move. But none were received. Under orders from Brigade the Battn. vacated the Billets in METZ about 1pm. & marched by companies to SOREL where they were accommodated in huts. The details rejoined the Battn. today.	
SOREL	14.11.17		The day was spent in re-organizing & cleaning up after the hardships & fatigues of the past few weeks.	
"	15.11.17		The Battn. vacated the Billets occupied in SOREL about 11am. & marched to a hutted camp in ROCQUIGNY, arriving there about 2.15 p.m. (See Move Orders attached.)	

Army Form C. 2118.

WAR DIARY of 1/04 R. Innis. Fus.
or
INTELLIGENCE SUMMARY.

(Erase heading not required.)

Instructions regarding War Diaries and Intelligence Summaries are contained in F.S. Regs., Part II. and the Staff Manual respectively. Title pages will be prepared in manuscript.

Place	Date	Hour	Summary of Events and Information	Remarks and references to Appendices
	15.12.17	11 a.m.	The Battn. vacated the billets & camps in ROCQUIGNY & marched to ETRICOURT where dinners were served.	
		2 p.m.	The Battn. entrained at HALLOY the detraining point being MONDICOURT. (See Move Order attached) Snow began to fall during the afternoon & on arrival at HALLOY there was a layer of about 3 inches on the ground. The march from to HALLOY from MONDICOURT was though a severe snowstorm. On arrival at HALLOY it was found that the Billeting Party had not arrived as the motor lorry on which they were, had found great difficulty in getting along the road. Capt. J. McMechan M.C. who had come by car had therefore to allot all the billets himself so that it was 10 p.m. before the Battn. had got into billets.	
		11.30 p.m.	The lorries with the valises & the Billeting Party arrived	
HALLOY.	17.12.17		Part of the Transport which came by train leaving ETRICOURT at 6 p.m. on 16th reached HALLOY early this morning. The remainder came by road, stopping the night 16/17th at COURCELLES-LE-COMPTE & reached HALLOY about 5 p.m. today. The day was spent resting & improving billets. Capt Boyce, 2/Lts Pickens, Nelson, Knox & 70 O.R's proceeded on leave to U.K. today.	
"	18.12.17		Snow still made all forms of traffic difficult & very little could be done in the way of training except clean inspections. Billets were inspected by the Acting Brigadier Lt. Col. Burnard during the morning.	
"	19.12.17		Under orders from Brigade the Companies on reliefs cleared the snow off a portion of the road between HALLOY & LUCHEUX today	

Army Form C. 2118.

WAR DIARY of 106 R. Innis. Fus.

or INTELLIGENCE SUMMARY.

(Erase heading not required.)

Instructions regarding War Diaries and Intelligence Summaries are contained in F. S. Regs., Part II. and the Staff Manual respectively. Title pages will be prepared in manuscript.

Place	Date	Hour	Summary of Events and Information	Remarks and references to Appendices
HALLOY	19.12.17		The undm Officers having joined the Bn. today are taken on strength & posted to Companies as follows:—	
			2/Lieut. W.P. Johnston A' Coy. Wounded 11.8.17	
			" G. Watson B' "	
			" G. Darling A' "	
			" C. Taylor D' "	
			" P. Hennessy D' "	
			" W.B Parkes C' "	
			" L.C.W. Steele C' "	
	20.12.17		The work started on the 19th was completed today.	
			The C.O. Lt. Col A.R. Lord Farnham went to England on 1 months leave today, Lt R.M. Boyle 7.2/R.I.F. M.G.O. on fourteen days leave. Major R.S Knox takes over command of the Bn. as from today during the absence of Lt-Col Lord Farnham, Major Z.H. Robin taking over the duties of Second-in-command.	
"	21.12.17	9am to 11am	Company Parades 8pm proceeded on leave. Severe frosty weather still continues.	

A5834 Wt. W.4973 M687 750,000 8/16 D. D. & L. Ltd. Forms/C.2118/13.

Army Form C. 2118.

WAR DIARY of 10th R. Innis Fus.
INTELLIGENCE SUMMARY.
(Erase heading not required.)

Instructions regarding War Diaries and Intelligence Summaries are contained in F. S. Regs., Part II. and the Staff Manual, respectively. Title pages will be prepared in manuscript.

Place	Date	Hour	Summary of Events and Information	Remarks and references to Appendices
HALLOY	22.12.17	9am to 1pm	Company Parades. Weather still very frosty. A draft of 130 O.Rs having joined are taken on strength & posted to Coys	
"	23.12.17		Church Parades.	
"	24.12.17	7am-11am	Company Parades. Remainder of the day was spent in preparing Billets for Christmas Day. Sgt. Fyfie having joined the Bn. on transfer from the 9th (N.I.H.) R. Inish. Fus. as Transport Sergeant, once Sgt. Cox, returned to duty, is taken on strength & posted to 'A' Coy. Extract from Battn. Orders:— The Corps Commander has awarded the Military Medal to u/m N.C.O's & Men under auty. granted by His Majesty the King. 19300 Sgt. W.H. Henny 'B' Coy. 9956 L/Cpl N. Joyce 'C' Coy. 27385 " J. Wilmot 'D' " 15858 " J. McIntyre H.Q. 15986 " J. Roulstone 'B' " 19878 " T. McElroy 'D' Coy 19124 " R. Montgomery 'C' " 23614 " S. McGonagle 'B' " 21202 Cpl W. Fleming 'C' " 15651 " S. Realy 'C' " 15518 " W. McClay 'A' " 27382 Pte C. Boyd 'A' " 15997 L/Cpl W. Shanks 'D' " 15996 " W. Shields 'B' " 15459 " T. Dinar 'A' " 19157 " A. McGowan H.Q. 19882 " B. Moor 'D' " 15584 " J. Harte 'A' Coy.	

Army Form C. 2118.

WAR DIARY of 10th R. Innis. Fus.

INTELLIGENCE SUMMARY.

(Erase heading not required.)

Instructions regarding War Diaries and Intelligence Summaries are contained in F. S. Regs., Part II. and the Staff Manual respectively. Title pages will be prepared in manuscript.

Place	Date	Hour	Summary of Events and Information	Remarks and references to Appendices
HALLOY	25.12.17		Christmas services during the morning	
		1.30pm	Dinners. Headquarters & each Company messed separately, the Officers & N.C.O.'s serving out a good dinner to each man. The C.O. visited the messes wishing all ranks a Merry Christmas. During the evening it started snowing heavily continuing to do so throughout the night. Major J.H. Barton proceeded on leave today, Capt. J.F.E. Miller taking over the duties of Second-in-Command during his absence.	
"	26.12.17		Owing to the heavy fall of snow during the previous night, the Bn. was again ordered to clear the HALLOY Road.	
"	27.12.17		The work started on the 26th was continued today.	
"	28.12.17		This work was again carried on. Bn. Advance Party of 10Off. & 50.R's proceeded to a New Area to take over Billets for the Bn. A portion of the Transport, & all pack animals & Riding horses proceeded by road leaving at 9.10am.	
"	29.12.17		The Bn. moved to a New Area arriving there at 4.45pm. (See Move Orders attached). 1 O.R. proceeded on leave today.	

Army Form C. 2118.

WAR DIARY of 10th R. Innis. Fus.
or
INTELLIGENCE SUMMARY.
(Erase heading not required.)

Instructions regarding War Diaries and Intelligence Summaries are contained in F. S. Regs., Part II. and the Staff Manual respectively. Title pages will be prepared in manuscript.

Place	Date	Hour	Summary of Events and Information	Remarks and references to Appendices
DEMUIN	30-12-17	2.45pm	Church Parade.	
"	31-12-17	9am	Clean Parades	
			Kit + Billet Inspections during the morning.	

Richard Hope
10751 R Dundalk? Lt

Army Form C. 2118.

WAR DIARY of 104 R Innis. Fus.
or
INTELLIGENCE SUMMARY.

(Erase heading not required.)

Place	Date	Hour	Summary of Events and Information	Remarks and references to Appendices
DEMUIN.	31.12.7		The strength of the Battalion today is as follows:—	
			Off. W.O. O.R.	
			With Battalion 35 5 545	
			Hospital 2 — 84	
			On Leave 9 — 28	
			On Command 7 — 46	
			Total 53 — 5 — 703	

10TH ROYAL INNISKILLING FUSILIERS.

WAR DIARY

for

MONTH OF JANUARY, 1918.

Army Form C. 2118.

WAR DIARY
or
INTELLIGENCE SUMMARY.
(Erase heading not required.)

Instructions regarding War Diaries and Intelligence Summaries are contained in F. S. Regs., Part II. and the Staff Manual respectively. Title pages will be prepared in manuscript.

War Diary

of

10th (Service) Battalion Royal Inniskilling Fusiliers.

Place	Date	Hour	Summary of Events and Information	Remarks and references to Appendices

WAR DIARY
or
INTELLIGENCE SUMMARY.

(Erase heading not required.)

Army Form C. 2118.

Instructions regarding War Diaries and Intelligence Summaries are contained in F. S. Regs., Part II. and the Staff Manual respectively. Title pages will be prepared in manuscript.

Place	Date	Hour	Summary of Events and Information	Remarks and references to Appendices
DEMUIN	1.1.18		The Strength of the Battalion today is as follows:—	
			Off. W.O. O.R.	
			With Battalion 35 4 548	
			Detached 7 — 45	JDL
			Hospital 2 — 83	
			Leave 9 1 27	
			Total 53 5 703	

Army Form C. 2118.

WAR DIARY
or
INTELLIGENCE SUMMARY.
(Erase heading not required.)

Instructions regarding War Diaries and Intelligence Summaries are contained in F. S. Regs., Part II. and the Staff Manual respectively. Title pages will be prepared in manuscript.

Place	Date	Hour	Summary of Events and Information	Remarks and references to Appendices
DEMUIN	1.1.18	10am to 12 noon	Short Route March. The Bn did not parade very far, as owing to a heavy fall of snow the previous night, the roads were unfit for traffic.	
			A Party of 10 Officers & 30 O.R. proceeded to AMIENS for a days outing.	
"	2.1.18	9am	Clean Inspections.	
			Under orders from Bde. the Bn. cleared the road from DEMUIN to VILLERS-BRETONNEAUX.	
			1 Off. & 9 O.R. proceeded to U.K. on leave today	
			Capt. B.W.L. Stange (Adjutant) proceeded to U.K. on 1 months leave today under A.I. 2327-1916.	
			A Party of 10 Off. & 30 O.R. proceeded to AMIENS for a days outing.	
			6 O.R. proceeded to 109th T.M.B. to be attached to them.	
"	3.1.18	9-11am	Clean Inspections & Company Parades	
		1-3pm	Inspection of Box Respirators by the Div. Gas Officer	
			AMIENS Party as usual	
"	4.1.18	9-11am	Companies on Rifle Range. AMIENS Party as usual	

WAR DIARY
or
INTELLIGENCE SUMMARY.
(Erase heading not required.)

Army Form C. 2118.

Instructions regarding War Diaries and Intelligence Summaries are contained in F. S. Regs., Part II. and the Staff Manual respectively. Title pages will be prepared in manuscript.

Place	Date	Hour	Summary of Events and Information	Remarks and references to Appendices
DEMUIN	5.1.18	9-1pm	Specialist Training. Rifle Range for all "indifferent shots" & company details.	
			AMIENS Party as usual.	
"	6.1.18		Church Parades.	
		9am	2 Billeting Party of 1 Off. & 6 OR. under Capt. Ritter proceeded to MESIERES to meet the staff Captain.	
			1 Off. & 7 OR. proceeded to U.K. on leave today	
			AMIENS Party as usual.	A⁸/1
"	7.1.18	11-12.30pm	The Bn moved to new area today. (See Move Orders attached)	
			Extract from Bn Orders No.8 :- The following list of decorations has appeared in the July Gazt	
			List of honours :-	
			Capt. & Adjt. C.R.L. Stacy - Military Cross.	
			Capt. L.M.H. Mark - Mentioned in Despatches	
			R.S.M. Scott L. - do -	
			The Field Marshall Commander in Chief has awarded the following decorations	
			Capt. R.M. Boyle - Military Cross	

WAR DIARY or INTELLIGENCE SUMMARY.

Army Form C. 2118.

Place	Date	Hour	Summary of Events and Information	Remarks and references to Appendices
	7.1.18		Lieut T.W. Cox. Military Cross.	
			2/Lt J. Mitchell do	
			" W. Price do	
			15572 C.S.M. Hamilton R. Distinguished Conduct Medal.	
			15364 L/Cpl Banks J. do	
BEAUCOURT	8.1.18	9am	Clean Inspections & Gas Drill	
		10am	B. proceeded to New Area to take over Billets for Bn.	
	9.1.18	8am	The Bn. moved to a New Area today arriving at 4pm. (see Move Orders attached) Although the March was over 17 miles not one fell out	
NESLE	10.1.18	10am	Clean Inspection & Gas Protection Drill	
		10am	B. proceeded to III Army Musketry School for Course of Instruction.	
	11.1.18	8am	The Bn. moved to a New Area today arriving about 3.30 pm. (see Move Orders attached)	

Army Form C. 2118.

WAR DIARY
or
INTELLIGENCE SUMMARY.
(Erase heading not required.)

Instructions regarding War Diaries and Intelligence Summaries are contained in F. S. Regs., Part II. and the Staff Manual respectively. Title pages will be prepared in manuscript.

Place	Date	Hour	Summary of Events and Information	Remarks and references to Appendices
	12.1.18		the march which was over 17 miles. We relieved a French Battalion & came into Divisional Reserve. Bn. accomodated in dug-outs in a chalk quarry. Dug-outs fairly comfortable but accomodation rather limited. Three officers went up the line & stayed there overnight. 10am. 9 OR. proceded to OR. on loan today	
Gd SERAUCOURT	12.1.18		C.O. & five other officers proceded to the trenches to reconnoitre today. The remainder spent the day resting & preparing to take over the new line.	
"	13.1.18	4.30pm	Final preparations were made during the forenoon for taking over. Reconnoitring parties proceded in advance to the trenches to take over stores etc. & find out the dispositions of the companies. The Bn. vacated the dug-outs & moved up to relieve 1st Bn. 119th French Regt in the line opposite ESSIGNY & URVILLERS. C&C. Relief orders attached. Twenty five officers including the M.O. & Padre accompanied the Bn. into the line, the remainder went back to a detail camp at ARTEMPS. Major Knox D.S.O. had command of the Bn. in the line. The relief was completed about 1.30am. on the 14th without any interruption from the enemy. Previous to & during the relief the French officers rendered great assistance & handed over their dispositions very accurately & carefully.	

WAR DIARY
or
INTELLIGENCE SUMMARY.
(Erase heading not required.)

Army Form C. 2118.

Instructions regarding War Diaries and Intelligence Summaries are contained in F. S. Regs., Part II. and the Staff Manual respectively. Title pages will be prepared in manuscript.

Place	Date	Hour	Summary of Events and Information	Remarks and references to Appendices
Battalion in the line	13.1.18		The dug-out accommodation was very good, but the trenches were not provided with dug-outs & were extremely muddy & in bad repair. The night was very quiet.	
	14.1.18		Very little artillery activity during the day. One French Officer remained with every coy. & the Captain with Battn. HQ. An interpreter & an artillery liaison officer were attached to Bn. HQ. The French artillery still covered our front. The day was very quiet. Steps were taken to improve the trenches etc. & everything got into working order.	
		4.0 p	proceeded to U.K on leave today from Transport lines	
	15.1.18	6.20 am	Enemy commenced a bombardment with trench mortars & artillery chiefly on the Bn. on our left, but partly on our left front coy. In reply to the S.O.S. from the Bn on our left & later from our left front coy the French artillery put down a good barrage	
		7.20 am	The bombardment ceased. Our losses during this bomb. were 1 man slightly wounded & 2 buried by shell fire & somewhat shaken. The remainder of the day was fairly quiet but heavy rain rendered the trenches	

WAR DIARY
or
INTELLIGENCE SUMMARY.

(Erase heading not required.)

Army Form C. 2118.

Place	Date	Hour	Summary of Events and Information	Remarks and references to Appendices
Battalion in the line	15.1.18		which had not been revetted practically impassable & great difficulty was experienced in getting rations to front line. The trenches being practically only slit-trenches fell in nearly everywhere & overland routes were reconnoitred to make it possible to take up rations under cover of darkness.	
	16.1.18		Fairly quiet day was spent. Received orders that owing to bad condition of trenches the tour would only last four days	
	17.1.18		The morning was again quiet & nothing unusual occurred during the day. The Bn was relieved tonight by the 14th Royal Irish Rifles, the relief being complete about 10pm. (see Relief orders attached) The Bn. moved into support & was accomodated in dug-outs about 2½ miles behind the front line. The accomodation was fairly good. 'C' Company had to remain in close support close up to the line.	
	18.1.18		The day was spent in having clean inspections, & resting after the tour. Some improvements were made in the sanitary arrangements & in the roads & trenches around the dug-outs	

WAR DIARY
or
INTELLIGENCE SUMMARY.

(Erase heading not required.)

Army Form C. 2118.

Place	Date	Hour	Summary of Events and Information	Remarks and references to Appendices
	18-1-18		Capt Davidson 9 S.R. proceeded to U.K. on leave today.	
	19-1-18		Quiet day. A Working Party of 100 O.R. was sent up at night to clear portion of the Communication Trench to the Front Line. Nothing unusual occurred during the day.	
	20-1-18		Services were held by the Pres. Chaplain (Capt H.J. Paton M.C.) in all the dug outs during the day. Some cleaning up was done in the afternoon.	
	21-1-18	6pm.	During the forenoon preparations were made for again taking over the line on the Right Sub sector. The usual inspections were carried out & the men's feet protected by whale oil against Frost-bite. The Bn. moved off & the relief was over by 9.30 pm (See Relief Orders attached) "C" Coy took over the Right Front sector. "A" Coy took over the Right Support sector. "D" " " " Left " " "B" " " " Left " "	

WAR DIARY
INTELLIGENCE SUMMARY.
(Erase heading not required.)

Army Form C. 2118.

Instructions regarding War Diaries and Intelligence Summaries are contained in F. S. Regs., Part II. and the Staff Manual respectively. Title pages will be prepared in manuscript.

Place	Date	Hour	Summary of Events and Information	Remarks and references to Appendices
Battalion in the line	22.1.18		The day was very quiet on our front except for occasional scattered shelling by the Boche on points behind our front line. The trenches are now much better than they were during our first tour. Wiring parties were provided to improve wire. 7.a.m. proceeded to U.K. on leave	
	23.1.18		Day quiet. Only occasional scattered shells from the Boche. Lt. Col. A. K. Lord Farnham returned to Bn. from leave 9 took over command from Major R. Knox D.S.O.	
	24.1.18		Quiet day. Inter-Company relief was carried out after dark without interruption from the enemy	
	25.1.18		Morning was quiet	
		10-2pm	Aircraft very busy. About 50 shells were thrown in the vicinity of Bn. H.Q. but no casualties resulted. The afternoon & evening were very quiet	

Army Form C. 2118.

WAR DIARY
or
INTELLIGENCE SUMMARY.
(Erase heading not required.)

Instructions regarding War Diaries and Intelligence Summaries are contained in F. S. Regs., Part II. and the Staff Manual respectively. Title pages will be prepared in manuscript.

[Stamp: 10th Service Battalion ROYAL INNISKILLING FUSILIERS]

Place	Date	Hour	Summary of Events and Information	Remarks and references to Appendices
Bn in Line	26/1/18		Major R.D. Rice D.S.O. &c. proceeded to U.K. on 28 days leave today. 2/Lt W.T. Morrison & 2/Lt R. also proceeded on a fortnights leave. Owing to a very thick mist visibility was very poor & artillery & aerial activity nil.	
do	27/1/18		Day was very quiet. Bn. was relieved by the 14th R. Ir. Rifles & on completion of relief moved into reserve at ESSIGNY Station. Relief was complete about 7.30 pm	
Bn in Reserve	28/1/18		The morning was spent in carrying out inspections & preparing for move in the evening	
		6.45pm	Bn. was relieved in reserve by the 2nd Bn. R.L. Rifles & marched to FLUQUIERES (see March Orders attached) Details from Transport Lines joined Bn today	
FLUQUIERES	29/1/18		The day was spent in cleaning up after the tour in the line, the Baths being available for the Bn. 7 O.R. proceeded to U.K. on leave today.	

WAR DIARY
or
INTELLIGENCE SUMMARY.

(Erase heading not required.)

Army Form C. 2118.

Place	Date	Hour	Summary of Events and Information	Remarks and references to Appendices
FLURVIERES	30-1-18		Clean Inspection & Parades under Coy. arrangements.	
			During the afternoon the Divl. Band played a few selections at a football match between C & D Companies.	
"	31-1-18	8.15am	Bn. paraded as strong as possible & proceeded to ROUPY to commence digging a new line of trenches.	

Farnham Lt. Col.
Comdg. 10th Roy Innis Fus.

Army Form C. 2118.

WAR DIARY
or
INTELLIGENCE SUMMARY.
(Erase heading not required.)

Instructions regarding War Diaries and Intelligence Summaries are contained in F. S. Regs., Part II. and the Staff Manual respectively. Title pages will be prepared in manuscript.

Place	Date	Hour	Summary of Events and Information	Remarks and references to Appendices
FLAUIERES	31.1.18		The Strength of the Battalion today is as follows :—	
			Off. W.O. O.R.	
			With Battalion 39 6 536	
			Detached 10 — 82	
			Hospital — — 37	
			On Leave 4 — 27	
			Total 53 6 682	

www.ingramcontent.com/pod-product-compliance
Lightning Source LLC
Chambersburg PA
CBHW080906230426
43664CB00016B/2742